LAKE OSWEGO JR. HIGH SCHOOL
2500 SW COUNTRY CLUB RD
LAKE OSWEGO, OR 97034
503-534-2335

People of the Ancient World

THE ANCIENT INCA

WRITTEN BY
PATRICIA CALVERT

Franklin Watts
A Division of Scholastic Inc.
New York Toronto London Auckland Sydney
Mexico City New Delhi Hong Kong
Danbury, Connecticut

For R.F.S.,
thank you for reminders of a time long gone

Acknowledgements
I wish to acknowledge the staff at my local public library, whose help in obtaining source material was invaluable.

Note to readers: Definitions for words in **bold** can be found in the Glossary at the back of this book.

Photographs © 2004: Art Resource, NY: 29, 45 (Werner Forman), 70 (Nick Saunders/Barbara Heller Photo Library, London); Bridgeman Art Library International Ltd., London/New York: 48, 52 (Archives Charmet), 69 (British Museum, London, UK), 31 (The Stapleton Collection); Corbis Images: 108 (Tony Arruza), 18 (Yann Arthus-Bertrand), 59, 114, 115 (Bettmann), 44 left (Gianni Dagli Orti), 86 (Laurence Fordyce/Eye Ubiquitous), 49 (Historical Picture Archive), 11 (Julie Houck), 15, 83 (Wolfgang Kaehler), 7 (original image courtesy of NASA), 62 (Scott T. Smith), 66, 67 (Roman Soumar), 77, 105 (James Sparshatt), 17 (Alison Wright); Mary Evans Picture Library: 95, 97 bottom, 111 bottom, 113 bottom; National Geographic Image Collection: 24, 28 (Stephen Alvarez), 12, 43 (Ira Block), 60 (Maria Stenzel); North Wind Picture Archives: 42, 64, 88, 89, 91, 92, 100, 110 top, 110 bottom, 111 top left, 112, 113 top; Panos Pictures: 4, 104, 111 top right (John Spaull), 37 (Tayacan); Photo Researchers, NY/Dr. Morley Read: 23; South American Pictures: 36 (Pedro Martinez), 76, 84 (Tony Morrison); Stock Montage, Inc.: 34, 81, 109 bottom, 109 top, 114 top; Superstock, Inc.: 97, 102; The Art Archive/Picture Desk: 87 (Dagli Orti/Archeological Museum, Lima), 72 (Dagli Orti/Museo Nacional Tiahuanacu, La Paz, Bolivia), 40 (Mireille Vautier/Archbishops Palace Museum, Cuzco), 26, 27, 56, 57 (Mireille Vautier/Chavez Ballon Collection, Lima), 47 (Mireille Vautier/University Museum, Cuzco); The Image Works/Topham: 65; Time Life Pictures/Getty Images/H. John Maier Jr.: 21; Wolfgang Kaehler: 33, 79; Woodfin Camp & Associates/Robert Frerck: 44 right.

Cover art by Joseph Fiedler
Map art by XNR Productions Inc.

Library of Congress Cataloging-in-Publication Data

Calvert, Patricia.
  The ancient Inca / Patricia Calvert.
     p. cm. — (People of the ancient world)
  Includes bibliographical references and index.
  ISBN 0-531-12358-8 (lib. bdg.)   0-531-16740-2 (pbk.)
  1. Incas—History. 2. Incas—Social life and customs. I. Title. II. Series.
  F3429.C22 2004
  985'.01—dc22
                                                              2004001956

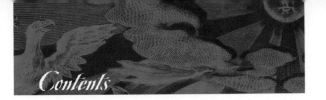

Contents

ANCIENT ORIGINS OF THE INCA

Thirty thousand years ago glaciers at the north end of the globe slid southward at the rate of a few inches each year. Landmasses under the frozen sea were exposed. One of them, a land bridge 100 miles (160 kilometers) wide, connected Russia and Alaska. In 2001, archaeologists discovered ice age stone tools and ivory knives in this region.

Hunter-gatherers crossed the bridge in search of plants and animals to eat. In small groups the first humans on the American continent drifted down through North America and into Central America. They couldn't return, for as glaciers melted and sea levels rose, the land bridge disappeared. The only remnant of this bridge may be the Diomede Islands, located in the Bering Strait.

Centuries Pass

Some groups settled along the way. Others continued their southward drift. Between 13,000 B.C. and 10,000 B.C., the immigrants' descendants reached the coast of South America. To the west, further travel was halted by the Pacific Ocean. To the east, travel was blocked by the snowcapped Andes Mountains.

Some wanderers established permanent communities. In 1979, archaeologists discovered a settlement dating from 13,000 B.C. in the pine forests of present-day Chile. Charred bones of mastodons were found in clay-lined fire pits. Digging tools, spear points, stone hammers, egg-sized rocks used as sling stones, and even human footprints were found.

A New Way of Life

The Humboldt Current of the Pacific Ocean provided South America's coast with what still are the richest anchovy fishing grounds in the world. Settlers learned to make bone fishhooks and build boats of *totora* reeds lashed together with ropes of braided grass.

People ventured into the foothills of the Andes Mountains to find other foods. They learned to cultivate wild plants, and by 4500 B.C. were harvesting squash. About 3800 B.C., corn was domesticated. By 2500 B.C., potatoes were second only to corn as an important crop. Between 3800 B.C. and 2800 B.C., cotton was grown. Llamas and alpacas were domesticated between 3000 B.C. and 2500 B.C.

From this aerial view, it is possible to see how tall the Andes Mountains are.

Ancestors of the Inca

Chavín This culture evolved from small groups of herders and farmers in about 1000–900 B.C. and lasted until about 500 B.C. Craft specialization began with workers whose only occupation was making crafts such as pottery, textiles, tools, and jewelry. At Chavín de Huántar, a ceremonial and trade center with an estimated 3,000 citizens, the bones of llamas, deer, and fish were found in pottery vessels. Images carved into stone buildings depict jaguars, snakes, and eagles.

Paracas This culture emerged about 700–600 B.C. on a barren peninsula that juts into the Pacific Ocean and survived until about A.D. 200. Information about this culture comes from burial sites where dozens of mummified bodies were recovered. Unlike Egyptian mummies, these were preserved in a sitting position, knees drawn up beneath the chin. Separate bundles of clothing, well preserved due to the dry climate, included fabrics, furs, and feathers. Many of the textiles were embroidered with designs similar to those used by the Chavín, suggesting an overlap between the two cultures.

Nazca As the Paracas culture waned, the Nazca emerged about A.D. 100 along the southern coast and lasted until about A.D. 750. It is noted for its exceptional textiles, for while earlier weavers used coarse llama hair, the Nazca preferred the finer fibers of alpaca wool. At the Nazca capital of Cahuachi, forty earthen mounds containing textiles stored in large pottery jars were discovered. Other pottery vessels held mummies seated upright, as were those of the Paracas. Fabric designs depicted heads severed from bodies, indicating that warfare was an important part of Nazca life.

Moche This culture evolved about A.D. 100, about the same time as the Nazca, but along the northern coast of Peru and lasted until about A.D. 800–900. One of the most important archeological discoveries of the 1900s was made at Sipan in the Lambayeque Valley, where gold and silver objects, shell beads, and feather plumes were found. The Moche, noted for their fine pottery, were the first of these cultures to build pyramids with steps. The tallest one is the 135-foot (41-meter) Pyramid of the Sun, while nearby is the smaller Pyramid of the Moon.

Tiahuanaca This culture emerged about A.D. 100 on the shores of Lake Titicaca, 12,000 feet (3,657.6 m) above sea level. By A.D. 500, this city-state had a population estimated at 100,000 and was distinguished by a trading system based on use of llama caravans that exchanged food, textiles, and pottery with distant neighbors. As the result of trade, this civilization spread throughout modern-day Bolivia, Peru, Chile, and Argentina. An artifact of the Tiahuanaca culture is the Gateway of the Sun, a huge gate carved from a single piece of stone.

Huari This culture arose about A.D. 600 in the Peruvian highlands, and reached its peak two hundred years later. The Huari terraced their hillsides, practiced fine goldsmithing, and constructed buildings in a style later perfected by the Inca. Pikillacta, a major city of this society contained seven hundred buildings, some of them three stories high, located less than 20 miles (32 kilometers) from what later became Cuzco, the Inca capital. By A.D. 900, for reasons not yet understood, the Huari abandoned their cities and returned to the countryside to live in small villages.

Chimu Based at Chan Chan, a government center covering 10 square miles (25.9 square kilometers) along the northern coast of present-day Peru, this culture emerged about A.D. 900 as the Huari declined, and prevailed until the mid-1400s, when it was conquered by the Inca. The Chimu were skilled weavers, potters, metalsmiths, and builders of roads and ritual centers. Most importantly, they designed extensive canal systems to irrigate the dry coastal lands where rain fell only every forty to fifty years. They were skilled tax collectors whose practices were adopted by the Inca.

The Inca: Children of the Sun

By A.D. 1000, several small tribes had settled in the fertile mountain valleys 11,135 feet (3,393.9 m) above sea level near modern-day Cuzco. In spite of having different languages and customs, they lived in relative harmony for about two hundred years. Between 1150 and 1250, they were joined by a close-knit tribe that was searching for better farmland.

The newcomers set themselves apart from their neighbors by their bold manner, and spoke **Quechua**, which they called "the language of free men." Their word *Inca* meant "lord," and the tribe revered its leader as the *Sapa Inca*, the "only lord." Today, Quechua, as spoken by the ancient Inca, is the most common native language in Peru.

Although the Inca intermarried with other tribes, they considered themselves superior. They worshipped **Inti**, the sun, and believed they were *Intip Churín*, Children of the Sun, destined to rule over their neighbors. Around A.D. 1300, they began to subdue other groups in the Peruvian highlands by forging peaceful alliances with them or going to war against them.

The way of the Inca was not to merely dominate, but to improve on achievements made by the tribes they conquered. The Inca improved roads, bridges, and irrigation ditches. They developed crop-storage systems to feed people when crops failed. They skillfully administered the economic affairs of an expanding empire, and kept peace among the tribes they ruled.

Understanding the Past

Why concern ourselves with a civilization that disappeared centuries ago? What does the past have to do with the present or the future? The history of humankind, beginning with its earliest origins, is the story of us all. As we inform ourselves about daily life, religion, governance, or any aspect of an early society, we learn important things about ourselves.

But how can information be collected if passing centuries buried the remains of a culture under layers of soil and rock? What if a civilization was "preliterate," as were the Inca? For although the Inca had a spoken language, they possessed no written language, and therefore left no written records for us to study.

Then it becomes the task of archaeology, or the study of cultural remains and artifacts, to uncover and sift through whatever evidence remains. Archaeologists excavate ancient sites. They reassemble fragments of clay vessels to determine their uses. Charred bones from the ashes of long-dead cooking fires are

The fertile valleys in the Andes Mountains allowed many cultures to thrive over the years.

We learn about the Inca from discoveries made by archaeologists. The Inca groomed themselves with combs (top) and tweezers (bottom).

studied to discover what animals were eaten and how they were killed. Dwellings, burial mounds, and human skeletons are examined. Tools, shreds of clothing, religious relics, as well as other artifacts are inspected. Archaeologists then reconstruct how a vanished people worked, worshipped, and died.

Although the Inca of Peru couldn't write about themselves, others did. Historians use the diaries, letters, and memoirs written by observers after the Spanish conquest in 1532 to gather information about life among the Inca. Through the work of archaeologists and historians, the vanished past of the Inca has been brought to life.

How the Land of the Inca Got Its Name

The word "Peru" didn't exist in Quechua. In 1522, a Spanish explorer, Pascual de Andagoya, landed on the coast of modern-day Colombia near the mouth of the **Biru** River. He was greeted by natives eager to exchange their gold ornaments for iron axes. Using sign language, Andagoya asked where the gold came from. "Biru, Biru," the natives said, pointing to the river. The explorer misheard and thought the men had said *Peru*, the name by which the land of the Inca became known.

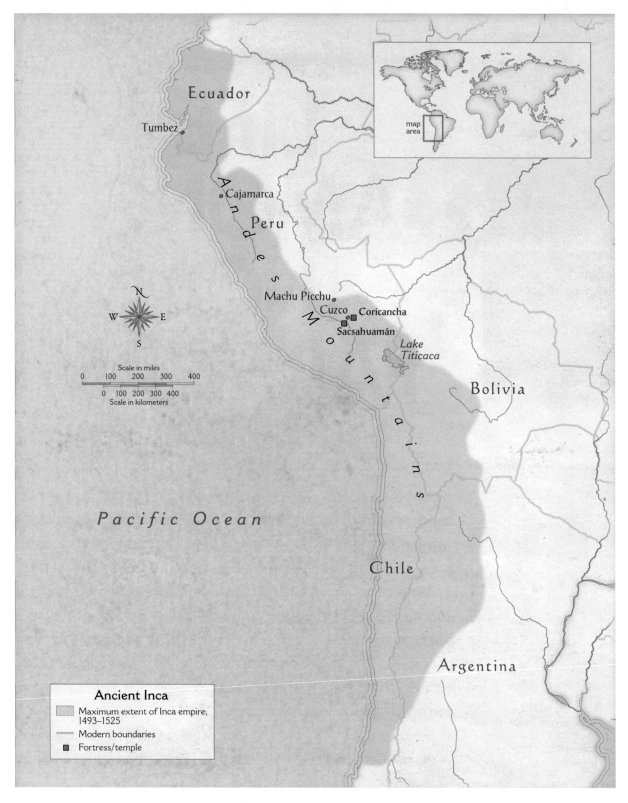

Ecuador

Tumbez

Andes

Cajamarca

Peru

Machu Picchu
Cuzco   Coricancha
Sacsahuamán

Mountains

Lake
Titicaca

Bolivia

N
W   E
S

Scale in miles
0   100   200   300   400

0   100 200 300 400
Scale in kilometers

Pacific Ocean

Chile

Argentina

Ancient Inca

Maximum extent of Inca empire,
1493–1525

Modern boundaries

Fortress/temple

map
area

LIFE AMONG INCA FARMERS

Chapter I

Because of the terrain, the Inca often carved farmland out of the hillsides.

As Inti lightened the sky behind the mountains, an Inca woman set out for a nearby stream with a clay water jar. While her husband and sons slept, she and her daughters joined other women from her ***ayllu***. An ayllu, or kinship unit, might consist of fewer than a hundred members or more than a thousand.

When the jar was filled, the woman returned to her hut and added sticks of wood to a small clay fireplace. She set a pot of water to boil, stirred in cornmeal, and added chili peppers for flavoring. When the porridge was ready, at about six o'clock, the family gathered around a blanket spread on the earthen floor.

As breakfast was eaten it wasn't necessary to decide what work needed to be done, for the choice had already been

made by the ***llamactu***, an Inca official. The previous evening, using a horn made from a conch shell, he'd announced to the ayllu which ***chacras***, or fields, should be tended.

Raising crops on the steep slopes of the Andes Mountains presented several challenges. The soil was rocky and poor, and droughts were frequent. Also, when rain came, it could wash away a season's crops.

The Inca solved the problem by carving terraces, or steps, into the hillsides. A trench was dug horizontally across the face of the slope, earth was piled above it, leveled, and then held in place by a stone retaining wall. The soil was fertilized with human or animal waste, including **guano**, or bird droppings hauled up from the seacoast. If a hillside weren't too steep, the terrace could be more than 100 feet (30.5 m) wide. In steeper places it was as narrow as 3 feet (1 m).

When the family reunited in the evening they ate a second meal. It might be a bowl of ***locro***, potato stew flavored with chili peppers and dried meat (the Inca didn't fry their food). At sunset, family members wrapped themselves in wool blankets, and then parents and children slept on the floor of their hut.

What Being "Inca" Meant

The ancient Inca used the word "Inca" in two ways. First, it identified the tribe known by that name, which ruled over other groups in the Peruvian highlands. Second, it referred to each individual in the empire. However, only descendants of the original Inca tribe were true Inca. All others were Inca subjects, but were not Children of the Sun, or of royal blood.

A Highland House

An Inca farmer's hut was built of stone or a combination of stone and clay brick. Its steep thatched roof was made of *ichu*, coarse wild grass that shed rain easily. Andean nights were cold, but fuel was precious; to conserve heat, the hut had no windows and only one door. The clay fireplace had no chimney, causing the interior of the hut to become so blackened with soot over time that it was as dark as the inside of a cave.

Planting Zones and Growing Seasons

The valleys of the Andes have three agricultural zones, each with specific characteristics. Inca farmers used the zones to maximum advantage, as do their descendants today.

Because the Inca Empire lay south of the equator, the wet season lasted from October to May, the dry season from June to September. When the farming year began in August, a festival was held to ensure a good harvest. It included dancing, singing, and the drinking of quantities of ***chicha***, or corn beer.

Extension of the Rocky Mountains

The Andes stretch like a 4,700-mile (1,432.6-km) spine down the coast of South America, from Colombia in the north to Chile in the south. These mountains, part of North America's Rockies, are formed of twin ranges called **cordillera** running parallel to each other. They provide the region with more than one climate. On the western edge, facing the Pacific Ocean, lies a desert so dry that not even cactus grows. Between the ranges, the climate of the **altiplano**, a treeless plain covered by sparse grass, is often mild. By contrast, snow never melts on the highest mountain peaks, 23,000 feet (7,010.4 m) above sea level. On the eastern slopes, rain-laden clouds from the Pacific Ocean release moisture, creating the jungles of the Amazon River basin.

Planting the Fields

Manco Capac, the "first Inca" of tribal myth, used a gold rod to mark the place where a new kingdom would be founded. At the start of planting season when it was time to sow crops, an Inca official—sometimes the emperor himself—commemorated Manco Capac's deed by turning the soil with a special digging

Agricultural Zones

Yunga	The lowest zone, below 5,000 feet (1,524 m)	This warm, dry area is suitable for cultivating a variety of fruit trees, such as avocado, lemon, and lime.
Quechua	The middle zone, above 5,000 feet (1,524 m)	This area has moderate temperatures and plentiful rainfall. Foods grown here include potatoes, corn, beans, squash, chili peppers, tomatoes, peanuts, sweet potatoes, and **quinoa**, a barleylike grain.
Higher Elevations	Above 10,000 feet (3,048 m)	This area is too cold for agriculture. Farmers used it as a place for their llamas and alpacas to graze.

tool made of gold. Men and women then planted the fields together, which were divided into thirds: One-third for the Inca gods, one-third for the emperor and nobles, one-third divided among the farmers themselves. Boundaries between the thirds were marked by government officials. If anyone dared to move a marker, he or she was punished.

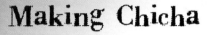

Making Chicha

Chicha was made by older women who no longer worked in the fields. They chewed corn kernels into a paste, then spit the paste into large pottery jars filled with warm water. The mash was allowed to ferment for eight days. Then the brew was kept cool by partially burying the jars inside a family's hut.

The size of a peasant's plot depended on the number of people in his family. A married man received one *topo*, about 43,056 square feet (4,000 square meters). He received an extra strip for each son, half a strip for each daughter. When farmers finished tending to their fields, they did charity work for widows, orphans, or those too old to tend their own plots.

The fields of the gods were planted first, followed by those of the emperor and nobles. Then peasants planted their own. Men turned up the soil with a **taclla**, a foot plow made of wood (sometimes tipped with a bronze plate). As the earth was turned, women knelt to break it up with their hands or a **lampa**, a small hoe. It was backbreaking work, yet men and women sang as they labored, to the amazement of their Spanish conquerors. "These chants are very enjoyable, and can usually be heard a half-league away," observed Father Bernabe Cobo.

Between planting and harvesting crops, many tasks needed to be done. Men repaired the stone retaining walls of the terraces while women gathered fuel. Nearby forests had been cut down to clear land for farming, so they traveled long distances to find wood. Dried dung (manure) also was collected from the high pastures where llamas and alpacas grazed.

If Drought Threatened Crops

If moisture didn't arrive at the right time and crops withered, rituals to bring rain were performed. Six llamas, only black ones, were tied up without food or water. When the animals' hunger and thirst became intolerable, they wailed in misery. The Inca believed the gods couldn't bear to hear such pitiful cries and would send rain. If none came, the llamas were sacrificed. If drought continued, human sacrifices, including children, were offered. Only when all measures failed did Inca officials open the **quollas**, or storehouses, to feed the starving people.

The potato was an important part of the diet of the Inca.

The Most Important Crops

Potatoes and corn were the Incas' two most important crops because they could be preserved easily. Potatoes were dried in the sun, allowed to freeze at night, and then dried again the next day. The process was repeated until all the moisture was extracted, creating *chuño*, or freeze-dried potato. This product could be

The Size of a Baby's Fist

Ancestors of the Inca discovered the **acsu**, the potato, growing wild in the Andean highlands and domesticated it about 2500 B.C. It was a dark, knobby tuber not much larger than a baby's fist, nothing like the large white vegetable of today. The Inca developed more than two hundred varieties of potato in colors including black, brown, red, and purple, and some were even speckled. Called **papa** by the Spanish, the potato was unknown in Europe until Francisco Pizarro introduced it after the conquest.

stored for four years. When soaked in water, it was ready to be used. Corn also was dried and then ground into meal.

The Inca ate no dairy products—no milk, cheese, or butter—for neither cattle nor goats were native to South America. Nor was meat a staple of the Inca diet. Meat, rarely eaten fresh, was cut into thin strips, dried, and then pounded even thinner between two stones. The finished product, called **charqui**, could be preserved indefinitely.

The **cui**, a small rodent native to the Andes (we call it a guinea pig), was the most dependable source of meat for the Inca. Guinea pigs were allowed to run loose in peasants' huts, ate leftovers from their owners' meals, and then became meals themselves.

An Ancient Drug

Coca, a 3-foot (1 m) tall shrub growing in the moist river valleys of the eastern cordillera, was cultivated after people discovered that chewing its tealike leaves counteracted the fatigue caused by working in the oxygen-thin highlands. A walnut-sized quid, or

Forgotten Manuscript

A Jesuit priest, Father Bernabe Cobo (1580–1657), came to Peru as a missionary in 1599. He learned Quechua and interviewed many subjects about their recollections of the old empire. He finished *History of the New World* in 1653. After his death, the manuscript found its way back to his native Spain and lay unnoticed in an archive in Seville until 1790. An English translation of Cobo's work, published by the University of Texas Press, is an important resource for students of Inca culture.

A Father's Blessing

Pedro Cieza de León was born in Llrena, Spain, in 1520. The arrival of shiploads of gold in Spanish ports stirred fifteen-year-old León's imagination. In April 1535, with his father's blessing, he boarded a ship bound for South America. In 1541, nine years after the fall of the Inca Empire, León began to record everything he saw and heard, filling hundreds of pages with observations now available to modern scholars.

wad, of coca was held in the cheek with a slice of lime. The acidic lime juice broke down the chemical composition of the leaves, releasing small quantities of cocaine into the bloodstream. In 1553, Pedro Cieza de León remarked on the native people's habit of keeping "coca in the mouth . . . from morning until they go to sleep, without removing it." Today, some Peruvians who work in the highlands still use coca as their ancestors did.

The coca plant, which is the source for the drug cocaine, grew in the homeland of the Inca.

Chapter II

GROWING UP AMONG THE INCA

As a baby's birth approached, an Inca father fasted to aid a safe delivery for his wife and child. After the baby was born, a mother cut the umbilical cord with her thumbnail or a piece of broken pottery. Regardless of the weather, she set out for the nearest stream to wash the infant. Ice-cold water was said to make a child's arms and legs strong, yet mothers often warmed it first in their own mouths.

Children Equaled Wealth

A miscarriage was considered a misfortune, because children who grew up to help their parents were considered a form of wealth. If a miscarriage seemed likely, a healer was called to prevent it. A ceremony was performed, including prayer, rubbing three fist-sized stones together, chewing coca leaves, and sacrificing a guinea pig.

Although children were highly valued, the birth of twins was an evil omen that required rituals and fasting to be performed to avert catastrophe. If a baby were deformed, it could be taken as a sign that his or her mother was unfaithful to her husband.

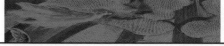

Caring for Orphans

Although children were highly valued among the Inca, disease or death could prevent parents from raising and caring for them. If other family members couldn't take the children in, they weren't abandoned to their fate. The government provided orphanages where they were fed and clothed. Eventually, orphaned children became property of Inca nobles.

Some peasants believed that if a woman dreamed of a snake, her child would be a boy. If she dreamed of a toad, the woman would have a girl.

Privileges Were Few

After birth, a baby was put in a *quirau*, or a cradle, strapped to his or her mother's back, and carried everywhere she went. Babies were breast-fed three times a day, but usually not more often, even if they cried. The Inca loved their children, but avoided treating them tenderly to prepare them for the harsh life that awaited them. Babies weren't given solid food until they were weaned at about two years of age, nor were they given names. The children were simply called *wawa*, or baby.

If a mother needed to put her baby down while she worked, a simple playpen was made by digging a hole in the ground to put the baby in. A pebble or stick might be added for entertainment, but play wasn't common for children who grew up in the highlands. By age three they often worked beside their parents at simple tasks.

Certain tribes flattened a baby's forehead, considered a mark of beauty. This was accomplished by placing small pieces of wood against the infant's forehead and tying them in place with a wool cord. To avoid causing the child discomfort, a mother tightened

Most Inca parents did not coddle or spoil their children. A painting shows a child being scolded by a warrior.

the cord gradually until the proper shape was achieved at around three or four years of age.

A Child Receives a Temporary Name

A *rutuchicoy* ceremony was performed at the time of a baby's first hair cut. According to Garcilaso de la Vega, the family's eldest male relative cut a lock of the child's hair and trimmed its fingernails. Other relatives also cut some hair and gave the child gifts.

Afterward, parents hid the hair and nails, for if they fell into the hands of a sorcerer, a spell could be cast on the child. The child was given a name, though not a permanent one. It might have something to do with the day of his or her birth, such as Thunder-on-Mountain for a boy, Flowers-Near-River for a girl.

Children in an ayllu were obedient because they learned three rules very early: *ama sua, ama llulla, ama cheklla*—do not steal, do not lie, do not be lazy. Thievery was rare, because not only would it be a crime against one's kinship group, but also against Inti, giver of all life.

Coming of Age

When she was about thirteen, a girl began her **quicuchicuy**, a weeklong celebration beginning with three days of fasting. The girl's mother bathed her, braided her hair, and gave her new clothes and *ojotas*, or sandals. A permanent name was given to her by her most important uncle, and relatives presented gifts. In return she honored the guests by serving food and chicha herself.

A boy's coming-of-age ceremony, or a **guarachicuy**, lasting three weeks, was more elaborate than his sister's. New garments were given to him. A llama was sacrificed in his honor, and its blood was smeared on his face. Relatives whipped the boy's legs daily to help him become strong and brave. He was given a *guara*, a breechcloth, and then took the name he would use for

Growing Up in Two Worlds

Garcilaso de la Vega (1539–1616) grew up in two worlds, one of nobility (his father was the Spanish governor of Cuzco), the other of royalty (his mother was the granddaughter of the tenth Inca emperor). Vega was attracted to his mother's people and called himself simply "the Inca." In 1609, his memoir of childhood, *Royal Commentaries of the Incas*, was published in Portugal. In 1688, it was translated into English, and is still an important resource for students of Inca history.

the rest of his life. It might be the name of his father or grandfather, or he could pick the name of a powerful creature in nature: Huaman (hawk), Asiro (snake), or Puma (lion).

After completing their coming-of-age ceremonies, boys and girls were considered to be adults. If they hadn't been chosen by Inca rulers for other destinies, they followed the work of their parents. If their parents were farmers, herders, or weavers, the young people became the same. Further education was frowned upon for most subjects, for Inca rulers believed knowledge encouraged people to question authority.

A metal sculpture is dressed in the clothing that was typically worn by young Inca women.

Chosen Women

Certain girls, including daughters of the nobility, whose beauty had been noticed by Inca officials, were selected at age ten to become **acllacuna**, or Chosen Women. Such girls went to live in a compound dedicated to Inti, where they took vows of chastity. Under the guidance of **mama-cona**, or older women, they learned how to prepare special meals and the art of weaving fine cloth. Later, a girl might be chosen as the mistress of the emperor, or, rarely, to be sacrificed to the gods. Either fate was a great honor for her and her family.

Chosen Women were guarded by sentries at the gates of the compound to prevent men from entering. If it were discovered that a girl had a lover, she was hung by her hair until she died, or was buried alive. Her companion suffered a similar fate. The dying words of two accused lovers were recorded by Huaman Poma de Ayala:

"Take me with you, father condor.

Guide me, brother falcon.

Take my grief and my affection to my mother and my father.

Tell them what has happened to me."

Time to Marry

When young women were between age sixteen and twenty and young men about twenty-five, they were called together by an Inca official who matched them up. Marriage was a duty owed to the empire. Remaining single wasn't an option. In the case of

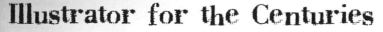

Illustrator for the Centuries

Huaman Poma de Ayala, the son of an Inca noble, adopted the surname of a Spanish army captain after the conquest in 1532 and learned to write and speak Spanish. Between 1584 and 1615, he wrote *The First New Chronicle of Good Government*, a 1,100-page manuscript now housed in the Royal Library of Copenhagen, Denmark. The document is important for its narrative, but even more for its 398 pen-and-ink drawings in which Poma depicted Inca daily life. Many archaeologists and historians borrow Poma's drawings to illustrate their own books.

persons with disabilities, they were paired with other persons with disabilities. For example, a person who was visually impaired married a person who was visually impaired, and a person who was hearing impaired married a person who was hearing impaired.

The couples usually weren't strangers to each other, for it was customary to be paired with someone from one's own ayllu. A young man and his parents walked to the bride's home, where her family gave their approval, and then everyone traveled to the home of the groom. The bride gave her prospective husband a wool tunic and a ***llauto***, a headband, then the marriage was celebrated by feasting, dancing, and drinking quantities of chicha.

The government provided all newlyweds with a plot of land, and they were expected to produce children. Inca officials, as well as peasants, viewed children as wealth. Rarely, a commoner took more than one wife (emperors always did). If he did, only the first was regarded as the "principal wife." Any other was considered a "secondary wife." If a man's wife died, he put on a black cloak and didn't remarry for a year.

Too Proud to Marry

An Inca legend illustrated the danger of refusing to marry. In **naupa pacha**, or in ancient times, Viracocha, creator of the world, traveled about as an ugly old man dressed in rags. He happened to meet a beautiful woman, Cahuillaca, whom all men desired. She refused them all. Her stubborness disturbed Viracocha, who changed himself into a bird and perched in a tree near where she sat weaving. He placed his seed in a fruit that grew on the tree and then dropped it in her lap. Cahuillaca ate the fruit and became pregnant.

After her son was born, Cahuillaca summoned the men of the village, for she wished to learn who was the father of her child. No one claimed the honor. She put the baby on the ground to let him pick out his father himself, but when he crawled to the side of the old man, Cahuillaca was repelled. She snatched up her son and ran toward the sea. Viracocha commanded her to stop. When she refused, he changed her and the child into stone pillars, where they can be seen today at the edge of the ocean.

An illustration shows a wedding between members of two noble families.

Chapter III

EMPERORS, TOP OF THE INCA PYRAMID

In the Inca creation myth, the god Inti rose from Lake Titicaca and created humans from the mud of its shores.

According to Inca legend, Viracocha, the creator of the world, commanded Inti, the sun, to rise out of the waters of Lake Titicaca. He knelt beside the lake and made several batches of human beings out of the mud, giving each group certain abilities. He told the people to hide themselves in caves high in the mountains and await his summons.

Viracocha called forth one group at a time and sent each off to live in places he'd chosen for them. The last group to be summoned were four brothers—Manco, Auca, Cachi, and Uchu, and their four sister-wives—Ocllo, Huaco, Cura, and Raua. Viracocha said they'd been left until last because they were Chosen People and could pick their own place to settle.

Manco carried a golden rod to test the soil as they traveled along. When the brothers and sisters came to a rich valley, Manco saw a **huanacauri**, a rainbow, in the sky. It was a good

omen, so he plunged the rod deep into the earth and named the spot Cuzco, "the navel of the world."

Viracocha predicted that his Chosen People would be ruled by thirteen kings. The earliest are probably mythical figures, not real men. Only the final six can be dated with certainty:

Viracocha Inca (ruled until 1438)
Pachacuti (ruled 1438–1471)
Topa Inca Yupanqui (ruled 1471–1493)
Huayna Capac (ruled 1493–1528)
Huascar (ruled 1528–1532)
Atahualpa (ruled 1532–1533)

Manco Capac, the first emperor of the Inca, is considered by many experts to be a legendary figure, not a real person.

Divine Descendants

An emperor known as the Sapa Inca, or "only lord," stood at the top of the royal pyramid. He was descended directly from Inti. He was the son of the son of the sun, going all the way back to Viracocha's creation of the world beside Lake Titicaca.

It was important to keep the lineage of the emperor and his family pure. Beginning with Manco Capac, the mythical "first Inca," an emperor married his sister. Marriage to close relatives, prohibited in most cultures, was glorified by the Inca, for it ensured that royal bloodlines remained divine.

One Wife, Many Wives

The emperor's sister-wife, called the **coya**, became the kingdom's official queen. Any children born to her and her

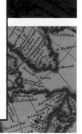

Society's Outcasts

All cultures have outcasts, and the Inca weren't an exception. **Huaccha concha**, "poor relatives," were offspring fathered by Inca men of royal blood, including the emperor himself, whose mothers were neither wives nor mistresses. Such children had no official place in society. Their best hope was to find a niche in their mothers' communities.

brother-husband were the pure-blood descendants of Inti. Their oldest son usually (but not always) became the next emperor. If a middle or younger son seemed more capable, he might be chosen instead.

The Inca also practiced polygamy, or the practice of taking more than one wife. Although the coya was the emperor's official wife, he was entitled to have as many "secondary" wives as he wished, by whom other children were born. In addition to his secondary wives, the emperor also had many mistresses, often selected from among the Chosen Women. Consequently, some emperors fathered more than a hundred children.

After an emperor ascended the throne, nobody was worthy enough to share a meal with him. He ate twice a day, as did commoners, but only in the company of servants. Seated on a stool, he was served from gold or silver dishes containing fruits, vegetables, duck, and fish. He ate with his fingers, for the Inca didn't use tableware, while a female servant held the dish before him.

If food fell on the emperor's garments, he changed into clean ones. If a hair were found on his clothing, a servant was ordered to eat it. If such a hair fell into the wrong hands, it could be used to cast an evil spell. Anything the emperor touched or used was

The first wife of the emperor was typically a close relation, such as a sister. An illustration shows the first wife of Manco Capac.

sacred. All clothing, uneaten food, or parings from fingernails or toenails were set aside and burned once a year.

To meet with the emperor was a great challenge. Interviews with the emperor were not easy to arrange, for he was protected by as many as 10,000 bodyguards. If a person were admitted to his presence, he approached with bowed head, bare feet, and carrying some sort of burden to indicate servitude. A visitor kissed his own fingertips, making smacking sounds to express reverence

Earning Their Empires

The Inca Empire contained vast wealth in the form of gold ("the sweat of the sun"), silver ("the tears of the moon"), jewels, and storehouses full of food, but new emperors didn't inherit such riches. The accumulated wealth belonged to the descendants of previous rulers. Each time a new ruler came to power, he had to acquire his own fortune. He set out to conquer new provinces, from which he then received tribute and taxes. This practice explains the constant growth of the Inca Empire. A new emperor couldn't tap the riches of his predecessors. He had to earn his own.

for the royal person. Female servants held a veil in front of the emperor to prevent the visitor from gazing directly at him. Every three or four years, however, emperors were carried through the kingdom on a golden litter (a seat suspended between two poles that were carried on servants' shoulders) to assure subjects of their living presence.

Even Gods Die

When the Sapa Inca died, the intestines (though not the heart or lungs) were removed. The cavity was stuffed with herbs. Then the body was dried in the sun until it became the color and texture of seasoned wood. When mummification was complete, the emperor's eye sockets were covered by gold disks, he was dressed in his richest garments and jewlery, and was placed on a golden throne.

The emperor's body was tended daily, as in life. He was offered fresh food and drink. Flies were brushed from his face. His clothing was kept clean. Amusing court gossip was whispered in his ear. When the queen died, she too was mummified and took her place beside her brother-husband. At festival time, these mummies, along with those of earlier rulers, were paraded through the streets of Cuzco.

Chapter IV

INCA NOBLES

While the emperor was the highest authority, he relied on his relatives and other nobles to help keep his empire running smoothly. The highest-ranking nobles in the kingdom were the pure-blood relatives of the Sapa Inca. They were members of a **panaca**, a kinship unit similar to the ayllu of commoners. It was their responsibility to administer the emperor's finances, pay his bills, and provide for his large family. They did their jobs with dedication, for they were part of the family themselves.

The lower nobility, relatives not of pure blood, were responsible for ensuring that work throughout the kingdom was carried out on schedule, and that the **mit'a**, or labor tax, was collected. These men became governors in the provinces or judges and priests. In return for their loyalty, they were given special privileges. The nobles didn't have to pay taxes and could take more than one wife. The number of wives a noble took indicated how wealthy he was, and his sons—those born to both the principal wife and the secondary wives— became members of the lower nobility.

A painting shows what an Inca princess might have looked like.

Taxes in the Form of Work

Mit'a, a Quechua word meaning "turn of labor," was a tax paid in the form of work. Male members of each Inca household labored for the empire for a certain length of time each year. Men served in the army, worked in the mines, or built roads, bridges, or buildings. During a man's absence, members of his ayllu helped his family until he returned.

Education Among the Nobles

The sons of nobles didn't automatically assume leadership positions in the empire. They were taught how to fulfill their duties by attending the **Yachahuasi**, or House of Learning, a university in Cuzco. At age fourteen, boys began four years of instruction by *amautas*, wise men. They studied the history of the empire, its laws, customs, myths, and how to use a **quipu**. Professional soldiers trained them in the art of war, the use of weapons, and strategic planning on a battlefield. When a student didn't perform well—no matter if he were a noble's son—he received ten blows from a wood paddle on the soles of his bare feet.

At examination time, students from the Yachahuasi fasted for a week, then raced barefoot up and down the mountains near Cuzco. They fought pretend battles with real weapons, which occasionally resulted in real deaths. Such deaths weren't considered tragic, but brought honor to the victim and his family.

Graduation took place in the main square in Cuzco. Young men were awarded a llauto, a narrow band worn around the forehead in which were fastened two feathers and a *canipu*, a silver disk. The size of the disk indicated whether the wearer belonged to the higher or lower nobility. His ears were pierced at a separate

The sons of nobles attended school in Cuzco called the Yachahuasi.

ceremony, entitling him to wear large earspools made of gold, silver, or wood. The spools were heavy. Eventually the wearers' earlobes stretched enough to touch their shoulders, causing the Spanish to call Inca men *orejones*, meaning "big ears."

Becoming a Royal Inca "by Privilege"

Men who were not Inca royalty were regarded as **yanca ayllu**, of common blood. However, a man could become a member of the royal class by privilege. Incas-by-privilege were created from political necessity. There weren't enough royal-born Inca to fill all the government positions in the empire. Therefore, personnel were recruited from elsewhere. Some members of the Inca-by-privilege

An Inca mummy
was found with a
feather headdress,
a sign of nobility.

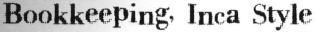

Bookkeeping, Inca Style

A quipu was a long rope made of wool or cotton from which dangled smaller strings of different lengths, dyed various colors with specific meanings: Yellow represented gold; white, silver; red, warriors; and so forth. The type of knot tied in the string indicated whether it meant units of 1, 10, 100, 1,000, or greater. Quipus could be carried from place to place. Everything in the empire, such as crops, people, and animals, was counted. Then the quipus were stored in pottery jars in Cuzco. If Inca administrators wanted to check past records, they consulted quipus that had been saved from other years. *Quipu-camayocs*, keepers of the quipus, were "not only the accountants, but also the historians" of the empire, wrote Garcilaso de la Vega.

These two garments were worn by people of high status. The one on the right is decorated with cantuta flowers, which were popular during Inca times.

class were chiefs from conquered provinces, or the sons or male relatives of such leaders.

Incas-by-privilege attended the university as did the nobles' sons, learned to speak Quechua, and were awarded a llauto. The inclusion of outsiders among the nobility served two important purposes. It was easier for the government to rule conquered provinces with the aid of natives from the region. Also, non-Incas who received privileges in the form of servants, extra wives, and exemption from taxation weren't likely to rebel.

Administering Justice

Stealing from fields or from the emperor's storehouses was punishable by death. However, local governors couldn't execute a thief unless they had permission from a superior. When deciding on the punishment, officials took the age of the criminal into account. Other than death, punishments included beating, blinding, and torture. Some criminals died in prison in Cuzco.

Administration of the Empire

The Inca were able to build a huge kingdom because they administered it so efficiently. The empire was divided into four *suyus*, or parts, each headed by an **apo**, or high government official. Each division was then divided into provinces of about twenty thousand households each. Below each apo were two provincial **curacas**, or governors, each in charge of ten thousand households. Below each curaca were two governors in charge of five thousand households, down to governors who managed only one hundred. An empire organized by tens, down to mere tenths, allowed Inca rulers to supervise the smallest details of life in the highlands.

Nothing escaped the attention of a governor whose only job was to oversee one hundred households. Thus, in an empire organized first by thousands, then several hundreds, down to a mere hundred, Inca rulers were able to supervise the smallest details of life in the highlands.

A ceremonial vessel shows what an Inca noble might have looked like.

Chapter V

INCA GODS, SPIRITS, AND PRIESTS

The Inca religion was the foundation of major celebrations and also guided all citizens, high and low, in the smallest details of daily life. Rituals, or acts performed at certain times in certain ways, were necessary to assure good crops, good health, and success in war for the empire. Every citizen did his or her part each day to assure the favor of the gods.

The Most Important Gods

The Incas' highest and most powerful god was Viracocha, sometimes called "Foam of the Sea." He created the world at the beginning of time. Although he was invisible, his handiwork could be seen everywhere. Unlike modern cultures that consider rocks, trees, grass, and mountains to be inanimate (not living), the Inca believed they were as alive as human beings.

Most importantly, Viracocha created humankind from mud he scooped up from the shore beside Lake Titicaca. He told some of the human beings they were Chosen People. The belief that a god made human beings out of common soil

An Inca priest
performs a cere-
mony to honor
the sun god.

will be familiar to readers of many faiths, for creation stories around the world are surprisingly similar.

Unlike Viracocha, who couldn't be seen or heard, the three most important gods who ranked below him were easy for the Inca to observe. Inti, the sun, was responsible for the health of crops. Without sunlight, everything would wither and die. There would be no grass for llamas to graze on, no corn in the fields, no fruit on the trees. It was important never to offend Inti, for his goodwill was essential to all life. Commoners as well as emperors

Tying Up the Sun

It was necessary to keep Inti, sustainer of life and crops, from wandering off. A huge granite outcropping high in the Andes near Machu Picchu was smoothed and shaped into a *Intihuatana*, or hitching post. The word Intihuatana is a combination of two Quechua words: Inti, which means "the sun," and *hutanana*, which means "to tie." About June 21 each year, a ceremony was performed to tether Inti symbolically to this post by an invisible rope. The Inca rested easier, knowing the sun couldn't get lost or be lured away by evil spirits.

began each day with a special prayer of welcome as Inti appeared from behind the mountains where he'd been sleeping.

Mama Quilla, Inti's sister-wife, was the moon. She was the mother of his children, the stars, who could be seen in the *llipiyac*, the "star-spangled night." Mama Quilla's custom of waxing and waning was the basis of the Inca nighttime calendar. As the moon, she would appear in the sky first as a crescent, becoming full as the month passed, then returning to a crescent.

Illapa, god of thunder and rain, made his presence known with his loud, booming voice. When the Inca heard it and saw bolts that he hurled like arrows toward the earth, they knew rain was on the way. Although Illapa could be terrifying, he was as necessary to crops as was Inti's warm rays.

Spirits and Holy Places

A holy place, a *huaca*, could be any site that came to have special significance to the Inca. An oddly shaped rock, a twisted tree, or the place where a stream bubbled out of a hillside could be endowed with special power. People visited such places and made offerings to the spirit that dwelled there. If a site was thought to have an especially powerful spirit, it was given its own priest or priestess to take care of it. Father Bernabe Cobo listed 350 such places in the empire. Twenty-first century Inca peasants still worship at some of them.

People consulted their ancestors on important matters, for it was thought that the dead influenced the affairs of the living. Each person also had a *hauqui*, or guardian spirit. Of course, not all spirits were helpful. *Uma purik*, or phantoms, lurked about, especially after darkness fell. People also feared being attacked by *masaruna*, men shaped like bats who flew about at night.

Being a Priest

The *villac uma*, "he who speaks," the high priest of the sun, lived in a special palace in Cuzco called the Coricancha. He was a brother or an uncle of the emperor, which meant he was related to Inti himself. His most important assistants were ten *hatun villca*, or bishops, each of whom came from a different section of the

Lesser Gods—But Still Powerful

The earth itself was the goddess Pachamama, or "Mother Earth." She was tenderly regarded by peasants who tilled the land, for she sustained their crops. Farmers also prayed to Mamazora, the corn goddess. For the Inca who lived along the coast and depended on fishing for their livelihood, Mamacocha, the goddess of the sea and all other bodies of water mattered most. The kindly god of the huanacauri, the rainbow, could be seen after a rainfall.

Predicting the Future

Priests practiced divination, the prediction of the future. One method was to sacrifice a llama and then examine its lungs or intestines for signs of what the future held. Everything that happened in the visible world also could be used for divination. The way a flock of birds flew across the sky, a cloud that had a strange shape, shooting stars, eclipses, or the cry of an animal in the night (especially the call of an owl) was "read" as a sign from the gods and interpreted for its meaning.

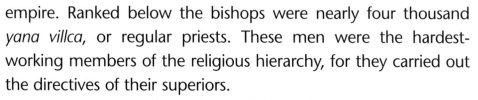

empire. Ranked below the bishops were nearly four thousand *yana villca*, or regular priests. These men were the hardest-working members of the religious hierarchy, for they carried out the directives of their superiors.

If a person had offended one of the gods, that god might take revenge by sending bad weather, disease, or other misfortune to the empire. To ward off such a calamity, the person was expected to confess the misdeed to a priest. To lie or try to cover up one's sin was a punishable offense, but once a confession was made, it was to be kept secret.

A penance had to be paid for the sin a person had committed, but priests took care that it didn't interfere with the work of the empire. A peasant mustn't be kept from his fields, nor a tradesman from his trade for more than a day or two.

The emperor and his blood relatives didn't have to confess to a priest. They confessed directly to Inti himself. Women too were part of the religious hierarchy. During the reign of Topa Inca Yupanqui (1471–1493), women were allowed to confess to other

There were many levels of priests in the Inca Empire, ranging from the high priest to the village priests.

Beneath the Ruins

After the Spanish conquest, the Church of Santo Domingo was built on top of Coricancha, the most sacred temple of the Inca. In May 1950, an earthquake revealed the original Inca building. According to Pedro Cieza de León, a stripe of gold "two hand-spans wide the four fingers thick" had decorated one wall, and the garden of the Coricancha was "planted with stalks of corn that were gold—stalks, leaves, and ears."

women. The structure of the Inca priesthood and the practice of confession were so similar to Catholicism that when the Spanish imposed their own faith on the Indians, it seemed almost familiar to them.

Temples of Worship

The Coricancha, or Temple of the Sun, in the center of Cuzco, was built to demonstrate Inti's grandeur, no less than the great cathedrals in Europe were constructed to honor the God of Christians. The gateway and doors of the Coricancha were covered with sheets of gold. Each morning in the courtyard, Inti was welcomed by the Chosen Women, each of whom blew him a *mocha*, a ceremonial kiss.

Many Gods, Many Festivals

The Inca honored so many gods that festivals occupied about 120 days, or nearly one-third, of each year. The emperor and his nobles, who supervised labor so strictly, considered the interruption of work to be worthwhile. Not only was it a way to satisfy the demands of religion, it was a way to reward peasants for their efforts. Festival days also were a way to bind newly conquered tribes to the empire.

The two most important festivals each year were *Capac Raymi*, marking the December solstice, and *Inti Raymi* in June, a festival honoring the sun. The Spaniards believed such events were pagan festivals and forbade them. In 1930, however, a feast day of the sun was reestablished in Peru.

Worship of Ancestors

As early as 5000 B.C., predecessors of the Inca began to mummify their dead, a practice that didn't evolve until 3000 B.C. in Egypt. Unlike the Egyptians, who embalmed the bodies of their dead, early coastal dwellers of what later became Chile preserved theirs by simply letting them dry out. Once the body was thoroughly dry, it didn't decay. In 1896, Max Uhle, a German archeologist, discovered the body of a twelve-year-old girl, sitting upright in a basket that had been made especially to fit her.

Heaven and Hell

Garcilaso de la Vega said that the Inca believed in *hanana pachua*, heaven, and *uca pacha*, hell. A person's conduct in his or her earthly life determined what happened after death. If a person went to heaven, life was very much like it was on earth, except he or she did not have to work as hard, and there was always plenty of food. Wicked people went to hell, deep underground, where they were always cold, had only stones to eat, and lived in eternal darkness.

Prayer, Sacrifice, and the Afterlife

The Inca didn't kneel to pray, as do many modern worshippers. An Inca stood as upright as possible, arms stretched straight out in front, palms turned upward. The person kissed the air loudly, then noisily kissed the fingertips to attract the attention of whatever god he or she was praying to.

Sacrifices to the gods could take many forms. For the most important events, a llama was chosen. A cui, or guinea pig, was acceptable for lesser needs, as were small statues made to look like humans or animals. Fruits, vegetables, and coca were common offerings. Fine clothing was appropriate, as were brightly colored feathers.

If a person had little to give, a pebble, a seashell, or an old rag was offered up. If one had nothing at all, one pulled hairs from his or her own eyelashes or eyebrows. A simple offering was better than none. As Father Cobo wrote, the Inca "used every possible way to show their devotion and affection" for their gods.

Incas prepare animals for sacrifice during a religious ceremony.

Chapter VI

HEALERS, MAGIC, AND DEATH

"Love of life is natural to all men," Cobo wrote, and "caused these Indians to look for ways to preserve and protect it from harm." The Spaniards, who regarded the Inca as savages because they weren't Christian, nevertheless "learned the healing powers of many plants."

Help from Healers

When an Inca went to a **collahuaya**, a healer, he explained where the hurt was located, and a treatment was prescribed. To flush out disease, purgatives (laxatives) brewed from plant roots were advised. Sarsaparilla, brewed from a highland vine (used to flavor some modern-day sodas), was recommended for curing sores. The bark of the **molle**, or pepper tree, was boiled and then poured into open wounds to speed healing. The place where a patient felt pain was rubbed with a garment belonging to the person, transferring the disease to the clothing, which was burned. Information about some of these treatments comes from illustrations on Inca pottery.

Why Were the Inca Called "Indians"?

Christopher Columbus believed by sailing west he had found a shorter route to India. In October 1492, he landed on Guanahani Island, near present-day Haiti. Convinced he'd accomplished his mission, Columbus called the Guanahanians "Indians." The spice kingdom was half a world away, but natives of the New World were called Indians thenceforth.

Uncommon Afflictions

Verruca, a deadly disease among Inca living at altitudes above 9,000 feet (2,743 m), resulted in purple warts that dangled like ripe grapes from a victim's eyebrows, ears, and nose. It was caused by a virus, and, therefore, folk remedies usually didn't cure it. After Pizarro's conquest, the Spaniards, who had brought deadly European diseases to the Inca (smallpox, measles, and typhus), died of verruca.

Uta, similar to leprosy, is depicted on pottery jars made by ancestors of the Inca. At the highest elevations of the Andes, **surumpi**, or snow blindness, caused eye irritation that could result in permanent loss of sight. To treat it, **matec-llu**, a plant that grows near mountain streams, was chewed into a paste and then applied to a patient's eyes.

Inca healers found cures to disease in the natural world around them. An illustration shows healers gathering medicinal herbs.

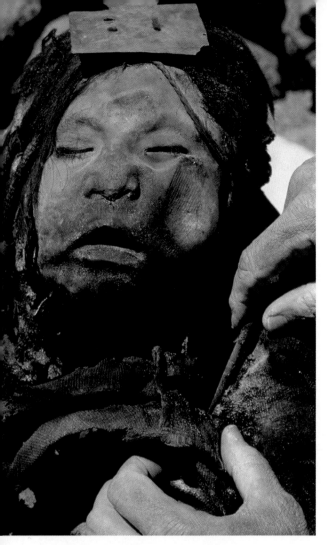

The Inca believed that sometimes a sacrifice was required to cure an illness. The mummy of a girl who was sacrificed was discovered by archaeologists in the Andes.

Commoners relied on the advice of local healers, but Inca royalty often called for special collahuayas who lived near Lake Titicaca. For hard-to-cure illness, sacrifices were suggested. A guinea pig or a llama, but sometimes a human—preferably a child under age ten—was recommended.

Medicine often was mixed with magic. A *hampi-camayoc*, a person who gathered herbs and powders to achieve cures, also performed sleight-of-hand tricks. After passing his hands over a patient, he held up a pebble, stick, or feather, identifying it as the cause of the sickness. He hurled it away, and patients sometimes recovered because they believed in the hampi-camayoc's power. In modern medicine this is called "the placebo effect." The recovery is attributed to a patient's mental attitude.

If patients complained of sore gums, roots similar to a dandelion's were heated and then applied to the inflamed tissue. *Sayri*, or tobacco, was used to clear the head. Moistened coca leaves applied to the temples could cure headaches.

Hypnotism was used if other treatments failed. A healer crouched in front of the patient, stared into his eyes, and cursed the disease inside him. Then he pretended to gather up the illness and carry it away. If sick persons were well enough to travel, they were told to go to a place where two rivers joined, for the Inca believed such sites were magical. Patients also were advised to bathe in water that corn had been soaked in.

Mysterious Powers of Blood

Bloodletting, a common treatment, sometimes was prescribed when a patient merely felt sad. The practice was most beneficial if blood could be let from a point near where the victim felt pain. If he had a headache, it was released from a spot between the eyebrows. Even dried blood was thought to possess curative power. For example, when a baby was born, the umblical cord was cut a few inches from his or her body. After the stub dried and fell off, it was saved and given to the child to suck on if he or she became ill.

When Bones Were Broken

If a bone were broken, the patient was told to return to the place where the mishap occurred and make offerings. The patient must have offended a god who lived there, who'd caused the accident. If the break included an open wound, its edges were cauterized, or burned, with a hot knife to stop bleeding and prevent infection. In twenty-first-century medicine, an electric cauterizing tool is used for the same purpose.

Human Sacrifice Among the Inca

The Inca believed disease and other calamities, such as drought, flood, and earthquake, were caused by gods who were displeased with human behavior. The solution was to appease them with combinations of ritual, prayer, and sacrifice of animals and even humans, if necessary. A child's pure spirit was the most precious gift that could be offered.

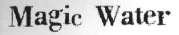

Magic Water

The Inca believed that all water possessed curative powers. Natural hot springs, common in the Andes, were used by emperors and nobles to cure disease or for their relaxing properties. In September 1532, as Atahualpa, the twelfth Inca emperor, rested at hot springs near Cajamarca, he received word that **suncasapa**, or "bearded men," had appeared at Tumbez, 350 miles (563 km) away. Soothed by the hot springs, Atahualpa wasn't alarmed.

Magic Drinks and Other Cures

A variety of liquids were used to treat disease. A broth made of hummingbirds' flesh was used to treat epilepsy. Another made by boiling the meat of a young condor cured insanity. Milk from a woman who was nursing a baby was prescribed for pneumonia. For poisoning, a lock of the person's hair was burned and the ash was mixed with chicha. If a patient suffered from headache, dental problems, sore throat, or fever, his urine was collected and then given to him to drink.

Coca was used to treat many illnesses. Juice pressed

The yucca plant was one of the many sources of medicine for the Inca.

A Secret Cure

Father Cobo reported that a shinbone of a nobleman's son was broken so badly that it poked through the skin. It was feared that the leg would have to be amputated, but first an elderly Indian respected for his skill was summoned. He walked to a nearby field, selected an herb, and crushed it between two stones. The juice of the herb was applied to the wound. Then a wool thread soaked in the juice was tied around the bone protruding from the boy's flesh. In time the bone disappeared, leaving a small hole that healed quickly. When asked which plant he'd used, the old man kept its identity a secret.

from the leaves dried up ulcerated sores or was swallowed to control diarrhea. Quinoa, a barleylike grain, was chewed to ease swelling in the throat. Leaves of yucca plants, softened in hot water, relieved the pain of rheumatism. Juice from an *oca* (similar to a sweet potato) reduced inflammation of the kidneys and bladder. Quinine, from the grated bark of the **quina** tree, was boiled and used for liver ailments, and seeds from the tree controlled migraines. Small amounts of tobacco, boiled in water, were prescribed for urinary problems.

If medicine combined with ordinary magic didn't cure disease, stronger magic, or sorcery, was required. The sorcerer cast a spell by making an object, usually a doll, containing something from the patient (nail clippings, hair, a tooth, even a lump of excrement). The doll was pricked by thorns or slashed with knives to drive out the evil spirit. But sorcerers also were feared, for they spoke directly to the gods. If someone died while in a sorcerer's care, the sorcerer himself might be killed.

When Surgery Was the Answer

Surgery, trepanning in particular—cutting a hole in the skull—was practiced with surprising frequency. Archaeologists speculate it was performed to release evil spirits that caused violent headaches or to relieve pressure after a skull concussion. Before the operation, a patient was anesthetized with cocaine or drank enough corn beer to become numb to pain.

Skulls discovered at Peruvian burial sites indicate that some persons underwent trepanation up to five times. Scientific examination of these skulls reveal that these operations did not necessarily harm the patients because the edges of bone had nearly grown together, indicating that they had time to heal.

An illustration shows an Inca skull that was operated on.

Curing the Kingdom

A *citua*, a special ceremony, was held in Cuzco each August as the rainy season began and people sickened because of the dampness. A hundred warriors gathered before a high priest who cried out, "Away with evil!" People sent up a cheer, whereupon warriors—twenty-five at a time—sprinted out of the city in each of the four cardinal directions, shouting that evil was being driven away.

People who remained in the city fasted. Each household made special bread by adding drops of blood taken from the forehead of a child between age five and ten to the dough. After bathing, people rubbed their bodies with pieces of the bread.

The following day, four runners were sent out of the city, again in the four directions. As they passed through the countryside,

Swift-Running Sickness

In 1524, **pahuac oncoy**, "swift-running sickness," struck the empire, cutting down nobles and commoners alike, killing an estimated 200,000 people in Cuzco. According to Huaman Poma de Ayala, people died so quickly that they couldn't be buried before condors swooped down to feast on human flesh.

people left their homes and shook disease out of their clothes so the runners could catch it and dump it in a river. The ritual ended that night as torches banished any remaining trace of sickness. Everyone celebrated by dancing and drinking chicha, confident that they were protected for another year.

When Death Came

No matter what kind of medicine or magic were practiced, death came to all. When it did, the body of the dead person was wrapped in a shroud—white if the deceased were married, black if not. No fires were lit in the home. Women cut their hair to express grief; relatives wore black to show their loss.

Men carrying the body to its grave moved at a trot, knowing the dead person was eager to begin the journey to the next world. A white male llama accompanied the procession, and then was killed. Its flesh was eaten later by the mourners, its hide used to make sandals. Earth was packed tightly over the body. Mourners jumped over the grave and then turned their shawls or jackets inside out before returning home. Each November, a three-day *taqui*, or feast, was held to commemorate the dead.

When someone died, the body of the deceased was moved to its grave in a funeral procession.

The Funerals of Nobles

The funerals of royalty were more elaborate, as was the preparation of their bodies for burial. Herbs were used to preserve the body, and the cold, dry mountain air accelerated the process of mummification. The eyes of the corpse were replaced with ones made of shell, gold, or jewels. Royalty were buried in *chullpas*, or funeral chambers. No bodies have been discovered in these vaults, for treasure hunters looted them after the Spanish conquest.

Eight days of mourning followed the death of a royal person. Sometimes a noble's best-loved wives, along with trusted servants, were entombed with him. Those about to die dressed in their best clothes, drank chicha until they became insensible, and then were strangled. The justification for such murder was that the noble's soul might refuse to go to the next world unless those he loved accompanied him. Archaeologists have unearthed the skeleton of a ten-year-old boy who went to the next world with what he'd loved best: The bones of a dog were found beside him.

Members of the Inca royalty were buried in special chambers called chullpas.

Chapter VII

WARRIORS, WAR, AND KEEPING THE PEACE

The Inca citizen-army was maintained through compulsory military service. Men between twenty-five and fifty years of age were required to serve at least once as an **aucu**, or warrior. When a man's enlistment was finished, he returned to his kinship unit and resumed whatever labor he'd done before.

The number of men (mostly farmers) to be taken from a single province depended on the size of the province itself. Fewer men were recruited from smaller regions to ensure that work in the fields wouldn't be affected. Men served in rotation. When fresh soldiers were needed, those who hadn't fulfilled their duty took the place of men who had.

A Professional Army
Although the Inca military was a citizen army, there was nothing careless or ragtag about it. It was a strictly disciplined force

A drinking vessel shows a warrior with a club and shield.

commanded by professional warriors who'd been trained at the Yachahuasi in Cuzco.

The army was organized in units of ten. For every ten warriors, a leader was appointed to train and maintain discipline among them. In turn, his ten-member unit was folded into a group of five others, commanded by a single leader. Two fifty-member units, or one hundred men, came under the command of yet another leader, until some commanders were in charge of ten units, or one thousand warriors. During the reign of Pachacuti (1438–1471), the Inca maintained an army estimated at 200,000 strong. At the top of the pyramid, commanding everyone below, was the Sapa Inca.

When a new province was conquered, its soldiers were taken into the Inca army, giving the Inca two advantages. The enemy was left with no armed force to cause trouble, and the total number of warriors at an emperor's command was instantly increased. New recruits found themselves still fighting, but *for* their conquerors, not against them.

The Inca army was highly organized. Every group of ten warriors had their own leader. An illustration shows Inca warriors in battle with the Spanish.

Feeding and Clothing an Army

The Inca army didn't fend for itself as it moved along, nor did it cause major disturbances in any province. Instead, the quollas, or government storehouses in each province, supplied food, clothing, weapons, or whatever was needed in an orderly manner. The provincial governor then submitted a bill to Cuzco, which was paid by the emperor's administrators. Foraging, looting, or interac-

Best of Three

Before the arrival of the Spanish, the Inca had the largest, best-equipped military force among the three ancient civilizations in the Americas. The oldest of those cultures, the Maya of the jungles of the Yucatan peninsula, mysteriously collapsed about 1400, for reasons archaeologists still debate. The Aztec culture arose about 1325, along the shores of Lake Texcoco in the heart of Mexico, and was destroyed by Hernando Cortés in 1520.

tion with a local population was forbidden. Thus, local order was preserved as large armies passed by on their way to fight in outlying areas.

In terms of clothing, Inca soldiers wore short, heavy, quilted cotton tunics, as well as vests made of *chonta* wood to protect them from enemies' spears and axes. Helmets of wood or cane (woven reeds) protected their heads. They carried shields made of wood or animal skins that were stretched and dried on wood frames, similar to the shields later used by the Plains Indians of North America. When close combat was expected, soldiers wrapped thick shawls of coarse llama wool around their fighting arms as protection against enemy knives or spears.

Weapons: Simple but Deadly

By modern standards, Inca weapons seem primitive. In the hands of their users, however, they wreaked havoc. The *huaraca* was a sling made of fabric or leather with a loop at one end that held a stone about the size of a hen's egg. It was frequently the first weapon used in battle. A warrior whirled it above his head and then released the loop, hurling the stone 30 yards (27 m) or more. Boys in the highlands used similar slings in their annual war against birds that ravaged crops, and some were expert marksmen by the time they reached adulthood.

In close combat, a spiked mace made of copper, swung on a short rope, could split an opponent's skull. The sharp points of a star-shaped weapon were capable of blinding an enemy. Because the Inca hadn't discovered iron, soldiers' spears were tipped with copper, bone, or wood hardened by fire. The spears of their leaders, however, often were tipped with gold or silver.

Sometimes the warrior might have a stone or metal head at the top of his club. Here are some of the types of club heads that have been discovered.

Clubs about 3 feet (1 m) in length, as well as axes with heads of stone or copper, were used in hand-to-hand battle. Javelins were hurled. **Bolas**, three stones tied to cords made from llama tendons, were thrown around an adversary's legs, crippling him long enough to render him helpless. Later, bolas were used to hobble the legs of the Spaniards' horses, making both horse and rider vulnerable. Such weapons, when Inca enemies had similar ones, were sufficient to wage war. However, they were a poor match for the steel swords and guns used by the Spaniards.

Military Strategies

A favorite battle tactic among the Inca was ambush. By hiding in narrow mountain passes, behind granite boulders scattered on hillsides, or among clusters of trees near streams, the Inca could be take an enemy by surprise. Because the Inca had no horses, one of a warrior's most valuable assets was his own two legs. How nimble he was, how swiftly he could advance or retreat in battle might determine whether he lived or died. Small wonder that during his guarachicuy, or coming-of-age ceremony, a boy's relatives whipped his legs to make them strong.

Crops and grasslands were precious, even if they belonged to an enemy, for they were a form of wealth. Nevertheless, sometimes it was worth setting fields on fire, then using the confusion of smoke and flames to overcome an adversary. Walled cities were common throughout the highlands, and laying seige to them could wear down an uncooperative province. Entrances and exits to the city were sealed to prevent inhabitants from coming or going. As food and water ran low inside the city, surrender was the only option. After the conquest, the Inca trapped the Spaniards in Cuzco, holding them hostage for a year.

Chaplains and Musicians Served the Army

Religious leaders traveled with the Inca armies. It was their job to bolster the spirits of their own warriors with daily prayers and rituals and to weaken the enemy by casting magic spells. Inca priests shouted insults and warnings, including the traditional threat to drink chicha from the skulls of the defeated. They also called on the wrath of Inti to demoralize a foe.

Armies in all times and all nations have gone to war to the sound of music, used partly to intimidate an enemy, partly to

Nowhere to Hide

Members of some tribes realized they had no chance of winning a fight against the Inca, yet were unwilling to surrender. They abandoned their land, burned their fields, destroyed their homes, and ran away. But there was no real place to hide. Such people were tracked down, and some were put to death as a lesson to others not to resist the will of the Inca.

inspire their own men. The Inca were no exception. As they marched into battle, tambourines rattled; trumpets made of conch shell blared; flutes of wood, bone, or reed raised shrill voices; drums set the beat.

When Victory Was Achieved

After a victory, Inca warriors who'd been especially courageous in battle were given rewards, among them extra wives. Vanquished leaders were dealt with harshly. They were beheaded, their skulls plated with gold and used as cups, as had been threatened. Their teeth were fashioned into necklaces, their shinbones made into flutes, their skins used for drums.

Although leaders of a conquered province were dispensable, the Inca didn't intend to destroy an entire population. Workers were too valuable to be killed. The victors' aim was to integrate them into the Inca way of life so the business of the empire could proceed peacefully.

Efforts to Avoid War

War wasn't the only means the Inca used to bring provinces under control. When the Inca decided to absorb a certain region, ambassadors were sent to the area with gifts and offers of privileges to local leaders as an enticement to give up without a struggle. If peaceful overtures didn't work, the ambassadors issued dire threats, which often did.

After a province had been subdued, a census was taken not merely of people, but of animals, crops, buildings, and anything that warranted counting. The new Inca subjects were allowed to pray to their old gods and maintain their language, rituals, and style of dress, but were required to include Inti in their worship. The efforts of the Inca to incorporate newcomers peacefully resulted in a stable empire.

Mitimaes: People from Elsewhere

If the level of discontent in a conquered province made rebellion likely, the Inca government resettled the troublemakers. An entire tribe might be packed up and moved to a different part of the empire already populated with law-abiding subjects. The ill will of the newly conquered people, called **mitimaes**, "people from elsewhere," was thereby diluted. As a result of resettlement, the Inca Empire became a patchwork of many different tribes, languages, and customs.

Chapter VIII

BUILDERS OF BRIDGES AND ROADS

Stone blocks weighing tons and pebbles no bigger than peas were more than simple building materials to the Inca. Everything in the natural world, including stones, rivers, trees, and stars, was thought to be inhabited by spirits.

Without Ruler or Square

The Spaniards at first refused to believe that the Indians had constructed the elegant buildings in Cuzco. The Spaniards' doubts arose from the mystery regarding "what tools and apparatus could [the Indians] take these stones out of the rocks in the quarries . . . without implements made of iron, nor machines with wheels, nor using either the ruler, the square, or the plumb bob [a type of tool]," said Father Cobo. Inca achievements were attributed to the "evil one," or the devil.

Made by Men

The most remarkable aspect of Inca masonry is how tightly the massive blocks of stone fit together, without any mortar.

Without modern tools, the Inca were able to create enormous structures, such as the buildings at Machu Picchu.

Garcilaso de la Vega observed, "you could not slip the point of a knife between two of them." The edges of some stones were beveled to further enhance their beauty, creating a building that was "a perfect whole . . . there is no detail that shocks the eye." Not only were such buildings beautiful in themselves, they sometimes conformed to the land. A barracks built on a steep hillside at Ollantaytambo proceeds in steps up the slope.

Although stones used in buildings weren't fitted with mortar, the Inca repaired damage to the walls with a sticky, water-repellent red clay called **llanco**, common to the Andes. The houses of peasants, usually made of a combination of adobe bricks and stone, didn't survive the centuries as well due to the damp highland climate. Yet in dry areas of the empire, a few of these simple huts can still be found.

The Craft of Inca Masons

To create a tight fit between one stone and another Inca masons used tools made either of harder stone than the ones to be carved or chisels made of bronze. Ancestors of the Inca had already used

Inca masons didn't use mortar (sand, water, and lime) to cement stones together. They cut stones to fit so tightly no mortar was needed.

78

How the Inca Did It

A Swiss architect, Jean-Pierre Protzen, studied how Inca walls were built. Then he spent several months duplicating Inca masonry techniques. At a former Inca quarry 20 miles (32 km) from Cuzco, he demonstrated how cobbles—small, black stones found in river beds weighing between 2 pounds (0.9 kilograms) and 20 pounds (9 kg)—were used to smooth the rough edges of larger stones until they fit together perfectly.

this technique in a building at Tiahuanaca, where the natural irregularities of a single stone, which measured 38 feet (11.6 m) long, 18 feet (5.5 m) high, and 6 feet (2 m) wide, were chiseled by working the top into a slightly concave shape. The bottom of the stone to be set on it was then chiseled into a convex shape, achieving a closer fit than if each were planed smooth.

Small, regularly spaced holes can be seen in the stones of certain buildings. These holes held wood or bronze pins used to attach solid gold plates to the wall. When the Spaniards dreamed of cities of gold in the highlands, they probably never expected to find buildings that were actually gold-plated.

The design of Inca buildings was the same, no matter their size. They consisted of a single rectangular room without interior walls, with a door positioned in the center. If a building were constructed on a steep hillside, a second floor sometimes was added that was entered from a doorway on the upper level. Steep roofs, the better to shed rain, were made of wooden beams covered with thatch, but haven't survived the centuries.

The shape of windows and doors in Inca buildings was unique. The openings weren't rectangular, but trapezoidal, narrower at the top than at the bottom. Father Cobo also noted that the stones weren't set upon each other in a precisely vertical manner but inclined slightly inward, probably making the walls more resistant to earthquake damage.

House of the Speckled Hawk

In 1439, Pachacuti, the ninth and most ambitious Inca emperor, built a fortress dedicated to Inti on the top of a hill called Sacsahuamán ("Speckled Hawk") overlooking Cuzco. The project took more than thirty years to complete, required the labor of twenty thousand men, and was a way for subjects to pay their mit'a tax. Such workers came to the capital from the provinces. If one became sick, another from the same province took his place. Inca rulers understood human nature: to reduce workers' homesickness, men from the same province were housed together in government barracks.

Pachacuti had Sacsahuamán built to honor Inti, the sun god.

According to Garcilaso de la Vega, Pachacuti's project commenced as four thousand men cut stone in a quarry roughly 45 miles (72.4 km) from Cuzco. Stones of various size were pried loose by wedging bronze crowbars into natural fault lines in the rock. Sometimes fault lines were wedged with dry wooden blocks, which were then soaked with water. The wet blocks expanded, widening the cracks and making it easier to pry the stone out.

The Inca had no oxen, pulleys, or wheeled carts to help them haul the stones

Tired Stones

Not all the stones made it from the quarry to Sacsahuamán. Some, called **piedras cansadas**, or "weary stones," were left along the way. Inca laborers said the stones had become too tired to continue their long journey from the quarry.

up the mountainside. A series of earthen ramps were built. Some of the stones were huge, weighing 90 to 120 tons and measuring 13 feet (3.9 m) in height. Six thousand men using logs as rollers and cables woven of leather and reeds hauled the stones from ramp to ramp up the slope. Once, a huge stone slipped, killing hundreds of workers below. Father Cobo observed the use of the ramp technique firsthand, for when the Spaniards built a cathedral in Cuzco, Inca workers were allowed to use their own building methods.

Garcilaso de la Vega estimated that one wall of Sacsahuamán was 200 spans, or 150 feet (45.7 m) in length. A span is about 9 inches (22.8 cm), the length between the tip of a thumb and the tip of the little finger of an outspread adult hand. "I often went to play at the fortress with boys of my own age . . . [but] we did not dare to go farther than the sunlight itself," he recalled. They were afraid of getting lost, for the building contained many rooms and narrow alleys that ran in all directions.

When Sacsahuamán was finished, it was dedicated to the sun. Only persons of royal birth, true descendants of Inti, were allowed to enter. At dawn, when the valley below was filled with morning gloom, the east side of Sacsahuamán caught the first light and was called **intip llocsina**, "place where the sun springs up." The Spaniards had no regard for Inca heritage, however.

The Sacsahuamán fortress is located northwest of Cuzco on top of a hill.

They dismantled Sacsahuamán and used the stones for their own buildings in Cuzco.

Bridging the Empire

Road builders throughout the highlands faced engineering challenges. There were many rivers and streams to be crossed, some flowing through deep gorges or across swampy marshes. The Inca never discovered the use of the arch and weren't able to use stone to span rivers. This didn't prevent them from getting where they needed to go.

If a suspension bridge was needed to span a gorge, stone pillars or sturdy wooden towers were mounted on either side. A pair of heavy cables made of reeds or ichu grass—Father Cobo said such cables were as thick as a boy's body—were attached to the towers. The floor of the bridge was made of braided branches. To ensure safety, cables and flooring were replaced every year. One such bridge, 118 feet (35.9 m) above the Apurímac River north of Cuzco, measured 200 feet (60.9 m) from bank to bank.

If the gorge was narrow, an *oroya*, a primitive cable car, was used. It consisted of a basket made of reeds, large enough to hold a man, attached to a heavy rope made of vines connecting one side of the gorge to the other. Men on one side pulled the basket across. If no basket was available, Cobo said the traveler himself was tied to the rope and then hauled to the opposite side.

Pontoon bridges, or floating bridges made of totora reeds, could be used to cross streams if the current wasn't too swift. Smaller streams were managed by placing narrow saplings across them. When a swamp needed to be crossed, a causeway was built using large blocks of stone to raise the roadbed above the water level. Stone culverts then kept the area drained.

The Inca built numerous bridges, such as this one, throughout the Inca Empire.

Roads to Match the Empire

The Inca built the longest, most elaborate road system of any ancient culture. They constructed more than 14,000 miles (22,530.8 km) of paved roads that have been often compared to those of the Romans. As was true of many aspects of Inca life, these roads traversing deserts, jungles, rivers, and mountains were improvements on ones built by earlier cultures, especially the Chimu and the Huari.

The lowland road along the coast, 3,000 miles (4,828.3 km) in length, began in the north at the Gulf of Guayaquil in Ecuador, ending at the Maule River in Chile. The highland road, also called **capac-nan**, the royal road, was nearly 4,000 miles

The roads built by the Inca were narrow and winding. They did not need wide roads because they did not use carts or wagons.

Chasquis: Mountain Messengers

The wheel was never discovered by the Inca. Therefore, Inca roads were built without concern for carts or wagons. Portions of the highland road were as steep as ladders and as narrow as footpaths, and included staircases. **Chasquis**, men who ran 15-mile (24-km) relays, used these highways to deliver messages throughout the empire, sometimes covering 250 miles (402 km) per day. This system allowed Inca emperors to be informed swiftly about what went on even in the most remote corners of the empire.

(6,437.4 km) long. It began near Quito, passed through Cajamarca and then Cuzco, on into high mountain passes in Bolivia, ending near Tucumán, Argentina. Shorter roads branched off the two main ones, creating a network that left no part of the empire isolated.

Inca roads were paved with stone. Large ones were set at intervals to mark the distance traveled. **Tambos**, or rest stops, spaced every 15 to 30 miles (24 to 48 km) included corrals for llamas. Caretakers at these sites kept corn, beans, and chuño available for travelers. For their time, Inca roads were as agreeable as modern interstates.

Chapter IX

FALL OF THE INCA EMPIRE

The Inca Empire collapsed almost five centuries ago. Yet the word "Inca" brings to mind not only a kingdom in Peru but the name of the suncasapa, the "bearded one" who crushed it. The bearded one is known to us today as Francisco Pizarro, the Spanish conquistador.

Pizarro was born about 1471 in Extremadura, Spain's poorest province at the time. He never learned to read or write, and worked on a pig farm as a boy. When grown, his future looked as bleak as Extremadura's landscape. Men like Pizarro sought better lives by enlisting in the Spanish army, but the pay was poor, and Pizarro didn't advance in rank. He began to pay heed to stories about a "new world," where riches waited for those willing to take them.

Quest for Gold

In 1502, Pizarro boarded a ship bound for Hispaniola, a Spanish colony. In 1509, he explored modern-day Colombia, then crossed the Isthmus of Panama with Vasco Núñez de Balboa.

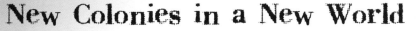

New Colonies in a New World

In the late 1400s, two events changed Spain's destiny. Christopher Columbus discovered the New World, and the Moors (Muslims), who'd occupied Spain for centuries, had been driven out. Spain turned its attention westward, becoming the first European nation to establish colonies in the Americas.

He settled in Panama, acquired land, and became the city's **alcaide**, or mayor—yet riches eluded him.

Pizarro joined Diego de Almagro in 1524 to explore the coast of South America. No kingdoms of gold were discovered. In 1526, he set out again, this time capturing three Indians who wore gold and silver ornaments and later became his translators.

In 1527, when he reached the city of Tumbez on the coast of Peru, Pizarro sent an emissary ashore to meet the local governor, who told of cities high in the Andes where gardens were filled with gold and silver flowers. Pizarro returned to Panama to recruit a larger force, but when the governor refused to provide money for one, Pizarro sailed for Spain to plead his case before King Charles V. While at court he met another explorer, Hernando Cortés. Pizarro listened carefully as Cortés told how he'd conquered the Aztecs of Mexico.

The arrival of Francisco Pizarro was the beginning of the end for the Inca Empire.

History's Witness

Pedro Pizarro, fifteen years old when he sailed to the New World in 1530, became his uncle's secretary. His book, *Relation of the Discovery and Conquest of the Kingdom of Peru*, is an account of the Inca Empire's collapse by one who witnessed it firsthand.

Man With Many Brothers

King Charles granted Pizarro permission to conquer Peru in Spain's name and gave him money to do so. Accompanying Pizarro on the return to Panama were his half-brothers: Hernando, Gonzalo, Juan, Martin, plus a teenage cousin, Pedro.

In 1531, Pizarro sailed for Tumbez with 180 men, including two dozen armed with crossbows and harquebuses (matchlock-style rifles), twenty-seven horses, and two falconets (portable cannons). He was joined by another Spanish explorer, Hernando de Soto, with a hundred men and additional horses.

On May 16, 1532, the Spaniards found the streets of Tumbez filled with rubble, buildings looted and burned. Inhabitants said a civil war had ravaged the empire. A new Inca emperor, Atahualpa, had seized the throne.

On to Cajamarca

In September 1532, Pizarro set out with 110 men and 67 horsemen to meet the new emperor at Cajamarca, 350 miles (563.3 km) inland. Although Cajamarca was silent when Pizarro arrived on November 15, Atahualpa was camped nearby with forty thousand warriors. Pizarro sent his brother Hernando forward, along

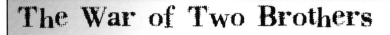

The War of Two Brothers

The Inca Empire might have survived Pizzaro's assault if not for the "War of Two Brothers." In 1528, Huayna Capac, the eleventh Inca emperor, died. By tradition, the emperor's eldest legitimate son, Huascar, would succeed him. But Huayna Capac favored a younger son for the throne, Atahualpa, causing the half-brothers to commence a civil war that weakened the empire.

Huayna Capac

with Hernando de Soto, to invite the emperor to a banquet the next day.

De Soto, famed for his horsemanship, knew the Indians had never seen a horse and put on a frightening display. He charged back and forth across the plain, then galloped straight at Atahualpa. He reined the horse in a few feet away, making the animal rear up. Atahualpa didn't flinch, but later he executed those among his nobles who had.

Atahualpa accepted the invitation. Then it was the Spaniards' turn to be afraid, for it was plain they were badly outnumbered. But Pizarro remembered everything Cortés had told him about the capture of Mexico's emperor, Montezuma. He too would be bold.

Atahualpa was seized by the Spanish during his first meeting with Francisco Pizarro.

A Golden Emperor

The Spaniards were astonished when the Inca procession entered Cajamarca. Hundreds of servants preceded Atahualpa, sweeping the way clean. Several thousand warriors accompanied their leader, who was surrounded by eighty nobles attired in brilliant blue robes. Atahualpa rode in a gold and silver litter. His gold necklace glittered with emeralds, and his crown was made of gold and silver. He wore a robe woven of gold threads and sandals that were made of solid gold.

Seizing the Son of the Sun

On November 16, 1532, the Spaniards rose early and celebrated Mass. Pizarro called his swordsmen to his side. Soldiers were stationed in shadowed doorways. Falconets were moved to a tower above Cajamarca's square. Everyone waited for Atahualpa's arrival.

And waited. It was late afternoon before the Inca emperor began his march toward Cajamarca. Then, to Pizarro's dismay, the procession halted. Atahualpa would continue in the morning, a messenger advised. Pizarro described the feast that had been prepared, stressing his disappointment. Atahualpa, ordinarily a shrewd strategist, made a fatal decision. He resumed his journey to Cajamarca.

When the procession halted, Father Vincente de Valverde greeted Atahualpa. The priest carried a bible and asked the emperor to lay his hand on it and promise to become a Christian. Atahualpa had never seen printed words before. He inspected the book and then dropped it to the ground. The priest stepped aside. According to plan, Pizarro waved a white scarf.

Cannons roared. Harquebuses blazed. Swords flashed. Inca nobles tried to shield Atahualpa as bodies piled up and stones in the square turned slick with blood. Pizarro dragged Atahualpa from the litter. Soldiers tied the emperor's wrists and ankles. Within an hour, two to three thousand Inca warriors lay dead in Cajamarca's square, and the emperor was a prisoner.

Atahualpa Ransoms Himself

Atahualpa soon realized the Spaniards were hungry for gold. He offered to ransom himself in return for his freedom. A room 17 feet (5.2 m) wide, 22 feet (6.7 m) long, and 9 feet (2.7 m) high would be filled with gold, "the sweat of the sun." A smaller room would be filled with silver, "the tears of the moon." Because the room was smaller, it would be filled not once but twice.

It took eight months to fill the rooms, allowing Atahualpa time to settle a troubling matter. His brother was still alive, but what if Huascar escaped, gathered an army, defeated the Spaniards, and then turned on Atahualpa himself?

Atahualpa hadn't been victorious in a civil war only to be defeated now. He ordered his brother's execution, which was swiftly carried out. Before his death, Huascar predicted, "I was lord and master of this land for only a very short time, but my traitorous brother . . . will wield the power he usurped for an even shorter time."

Freedom Denied

After the rooms Atahualpa promised to fill were overflowing, the emperor expected to be freed. But Pizarro had observed how the Inca revered their leader. His own force was pitifully small and could be overwhelmed at any moment. While Atahualpa lived, the Spanish conquest would be in danger.

Another Promise

Atahualpa bargained again, promising to fill more rooms with treasure. Pedro Pizarro noted that his uncle had grown fond of Atahualpa, and tears came to Pizarro's eyes as he refused the emperor's pleas. Huascar's prediction came true.

Yet according to Spanish law, the execution of any ruler, even a heathen emperor, was a serious matter. An excuse was needed. Unwittingly, Atahualpa himself provided one. Among lesser crimes, such as possessing many wives, which was contrary to Christian law, Atahualpa was charged with Huascar's murder and sentenced to be burned at the stake.

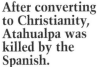

After converting to Christianity, Atahualpa was killed by the Spanish.

Measuring an Emperor's Ransom

Atahualpa's ransom weighed 13,420 pounds (6,087.2 kg), nearly 7 tons. After "the king's fifth" was set aside (the portion owed to King Charles V), the rest was divided in shares. Foot soldiers got a single share, worth about $300,000. Cavalrymen received two shares, or $600,000 each. Spanish farmers earned $25 a year, making Pizarro's men wealthy beyond belief. Pizarro got thirteen shares, worth more than $4 million. The man who'd once worked on a pig farm was finally rich.

It wasn't the prospect of death that horrified Atahualpa, but his sentence. To be burned at the stake was a horrible fate in the Inca mind, for a burned body couldn't be embalmed according to custom. Father Valverde offered Atahualpa a solution. If he agreed to become a Christian, he would be strangled instead. Atahualpa accepted and was baptized in the Catholic faith.

On Saturday, August 29, 1533, the Spaniards sang hymns as evening fell. Atahualpa sat on a low stool, and a noose was placed around his neck. He was garroted, his body left in the square overnight so the Inca would know their emperor's fate.

THE INCA AFTER THE CONQUEST

"Once the two kings, Huascar and Atahualpa, who were brothers as well as enemies were dead . . . the Indians [were] like sheep without a shepherd," wrote Garcilaso de la Vega. Yet if Pizarro believed the empire would collapse easily, he was mistaken. Inca nobles remained loyal to the memory of one or the other emperor.

Pizarro named Tupac Hualpa to take Atahualpa's place, believing he'd be a perfect "puppet emperor." The puppet's reign was short. He died of poisoning, possibly administered by Huascar's loyal servants. When Manco Inca Yupanqui (named after the mythical "first Inca") stepped forward, Pizarro accepted him in Tupac Hualpa's place.

Marching to Cuzco

In September 1533, the Spaniards headed for Cuzco, expecting to find more treasure. Along the way, five cavalrymen

Manco Inca Yupanqui proved to be a more challenging ruler than the Spanish anticipated.

were attacked and beheaded, and their horses were killed. Inca warriors cut off the animals' tails and waved the bloody trophies aloft to taunt the conquistadors.

On November 13, Manco Inca was crowned in Cuzco, and a celebration was held, but he discovered he'd made a bad bargain. The Spaniards proceeded to ravage the sacred temples and strip gold from government buildings. Pedro Pizarro, no more than a boy, took ten slabs of pure silver, each 20 feet (51 cm) long, 12 inches (30 cm) wide, 3 inches (8 cm) thick.

In January 1535, Pizarro built a new city near the mouth of the Rímac River. He called it *El Ciudad de los Reyes*, the City of the Kings, in honor of the three wise men present at Jesus's birth. The Spaniards pronounced the name of the river "Lima," as the capital of Peru is known today.

Born to Conquer, Not to Govern

Pizarro and his brothers were gold-hungry adventurers from Spain's poorest province. They weren't prepared to govern themselves wisely, much less the empire they'd conquered. Their crimes against the Inca would have led to their execution in Spain, but far from the eyes of the royal court, they committed barbaric acts.

The Inca were murdered, enslaved, their wives and daughters assaulted. When Gonzalo Pizarro took a fancy to Cura Ocllo, the new emperor's sister-wife, he seized her for his own. Later, she was killed, her body put in a basket and floated downriver for Manco Inca to find.

Manco Inca vowed to avenge Cura Ocllo's murder, for according to Inca belief, she was more than an ordinary wife. She was a child of the sun whose blood was as pure as his own. He sent chasquis throughout the empire, calling warriors to arms. Then in

Against Spanish Cruelty

Not all Spaniards in the New World were murderers. Twenty-four-year-old Bartholome de Las Casas went to Hispaniola in 1498 seeking a fortune, as did many of his countrymen. Instead, Casas saw the Spanish commit crimes against the Indians, which inspired him to become a Dominican priest. He aroused the conscience of the royal court in *The Very Brief Relation of the Destruction of the Indies*, in which he strongly criticized the Spaniards' treatment of the Indians and said it deserved God's punishment.

April 1536, Manco Inca sneaked out of Cuzco after telling Hernando and Juan Pizarro to meet him in the mountains, where he'd lead them to caves filled with gold.

Days passed before the Pizarros realized they'd been tricked. On their return to Cuzco they noticed the countryside was oddly deserted, but as soon as they entered the city, tens of thousands of Inca warriors surrounded it. "So numerous were the [Indian] troops that they covered the fields . . . for two miles around this city," Pedro Pizarro recalled. "At night there were so many fires it looked like nothing other than a very serene sky full of stars."

Seige: Time-Tested Inca Strategy

On May 6, 1536, with an army estimated at 100,000 to 200,000, Manco Inca began a seige of Cuzco that lasted a year. Roofs on buildings were set afire, which created heavy smoke that prevented Spanish counterattacks. Juan Pizarro died after being struck on the head by a stone.

Although Manco Inca had tens of thousands of men, many were poorly trained and starving. At the end of a year, the

Angered by the murder of his wife, Manco Inca Yupanqui led a revolt against the Spanish.

Spaniards' tiny force of fewer than two hundred soldiers hadn't been dislodged. Manco Inca retreated to the jungles near Vilcabamba on the eastern cordillera, where he later was murdered by the Spaniards.

Conquerors Attack Each Other

Diego de Almagro, with whom Pizarro explored the coast of South America in 1524, distrusted the Pizarros, especially Francisco. After an argument about how to split Cuzco's wealth, Almagro captured Hernando and Gonzalo. His followers urged him to kill the brothers, but Almagro tried again to strike a bargain with

Francisco. They met and pledged friendship. Then Almagro released Hernando and Gonzalo. The moment they were freed, Francisco seized Almagro and ordered his execution.

A King's Displeasure

King Charles V, angered by Almagro's execution because it wasn't sanctioned by Spanish courts, sent a trusted advisor to Peru to discover what was going on. The king suspected Pizarro of setting himself up as the ruler of "New Spain." Before the advisor arrived, however, the problem was resolved.

On Sunday morning, June 26, 1541, as Francisco and his brother Martin returned from mass, they were attacked by Almagro's followers. Martin was killed first. Before dying, seventy-year-old Francisco dipped his fingers in his own blood to make the sign of the cross.

Gonzalo, the Last Pizarro

Gonzalo Pizarro soon became as powerful as Francisco had been. In another effort to set things straight, King Charles V sent Father Pedro de la Gasca to Peru. Gonzalo wasn't alarmed, for the priest was a small, thin, soft-spoken man. When Gonzalo didn't cooperate, however, Father Pedro suspended the law of the land, offered pardons to those who had committed trea-son against Spain, and seized control of the country.

Gonzalo refused to accept a pardon. In April 1548, de la Gasca led an army against the last Pizarro. After Gonzalo surrendered, he was found guilty of treason and beheaded. His palace was destroyed, the land around it spread with salt so nothing would grow, marking it a place where a traitor had lived.

The Fate of the Inca

Inca workers had been valued members of the empire when it was ruled by the Children of the Sun. They were entitled to certain privileges, including plots of land on which to grow their own crops. Servitude under the Spaniards was far different. The Indians' plots were seized, and they were enslaved. The ***encomienda***,

Once they had been conquered by the Spanish, the Inca became slaves with no rights or privileges.

or plantation system, awarded large tracts of land to Spaniards for the production of sugar and tobacco, both in demand in Europe. Indians, who were regarded as no better than animals, died by the thousands under the brutal conditions of forced labor. A population once estimated at twelve million was cut in half.

As the labor pool of Indians became insufficient to work the fields, slaves were imported from Africa. Quantities of gold and silver were needed in Europe for the art projects of the Renaissance, requiring even greater numbers of Africans to work in the mines of the eastern cordillera. As the races mixed—Indian, Spanish, and African—a **mestizo**, or mixed-race population, emerged in Peru.

Finding a Lost City

For years, tales circulated in Peru about a mysterious city so high in the Andes that it was always hidden by clouds. It was said to have been built in about 1450 by Pachacuti, the ninth Inca emperor. After the Spanish invasion, Inca royalty—including Manco Inca—supposedly hid gold at Machu Picchu ("Old Peak"). In 1875, Charles Weiner, a French explorer, searched for the city without success.

In 1911, thirty-five-year-old Hiram Bingham, a professor at Yale University, heard such stories and traveled to Peru. Melchor Arteaga, a tavernkeeper, told Bingham where the city might be located. The professor paid Arteaga a silver dollar—four times the man's daily wage—and began his search on July 24, 1911.

The day was cold and drizzly. Bingham crawled on his hands and knees across a precarious bridge—spindly saplings lashed together with vines—spanning the Urubamba River, about 50 miles (80 km) northwest of Cuzco. He climbed up the mountain-

Machu Picchu stands today as a monument to its Inca builders and the culture that developed there.

side to an elevation of 10,000 feet (3,048 m). Suddenly, he came upon a city of more than two hundred buildings obscured by vines, moss, and bamboo thickets.

In 1912, Bingham returned with *National Geographic* experts to explore and map the site. Today, Machu Picchu can be reached easily by rail. The Inca city, lost for centuries, is visited by tens of thousands of tourists from all parts of the world eager to catch a glimpse of the ancient past and imagine what life among the Children of the Sun was like.

Chapter XI

LEGACY OF THE INCA

Much of the homeland of the Inca forms modern-day Peru, the third largest country in South America (after Argentina and Brazil). Peru achieved independence from Spain in 1824, nearly three hundred years after the fall of the Inca Empire. Its population of about 26 million people is more than twice that of Inca times. Nearly 90 percent of citizens are Catholic. Only 15 percent of the population is white. The rest is 45 percent Indian, 37 percent mestizo (mixed-race), and 3 percent black and Asian. The country has two official languages: Spanish and Quechua, the ancient language of the highlands.

Wealth and Poverty

The Humboldt Current, which gave South American ice-age emigrants their first dependable food source, still provides Peru with the world's largest fish catch. Despite periods of overfishing and the impact of El Niño (a climate change that disrupts the Humboldt Current), exports of shrimp, anchovy, and fish meal (fertilizer) equal more than $1 billion a year.

Petroleum, gold, tin, copper, coffee, lumber, and

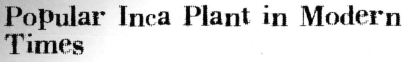

Popular Inca Plant in Modern Times

Modern doctors use cocaine, derived from coca leaves, as an anesthetic. In a nation whose farmers are desperately poor, growing coca intended for the illegal drug trade is often a way to improve their living standard. The value of coca as an export is estimated to be more than all other exports combined. About 741,000 acres (300,100 hectares) of land are devoted to coca cultivation, accounting for 60 percent of the world's supply. As many as 200,000 Peruvians are engaged in some aspect of growing, refining, or distributing coca. Crime and social instability are the inevitable by-products of such activity.

tobacco exported to the United States, Britain, Germany, and Japan amount to $7.1 billion per year. However, the majority of Peruvian workers are engaged in agriculture and are desperately poor. Rural homes usually have no electricity, running water, or sewage systems. People who migrate to the cities hoping for a better life often find themselves living in *pueblos jóvenes*, or shantytowns, where conditions are equally difficult.

Arts and Music

The skills of Inca goldsmiths and silversmiths, potters, weavers, and sculptors have been preserved by modern Peruvian artisans. Their work is sought by art galleries around the world, and ordinary travelers to Peru can purchase pieces at open-air markets. *Música folklórica*, traditional folk music played on the *charango*, a small mandolin, and the *antara*, panpipes, is played on the streets and in cafes. Although the Inca had no alphabet and didn't write about themselves, today, Peruvian authors such as Mario Vargas

Llosa are admired wherever good books are read. Novels written in Quechua describe life among the *Indigenistas,* or native people.

Peru's Future

Cultural divisions that began with the Spanish conquest have given rise to revolutions and guerilla movements in modern Peru. In the 1990s, government efforts to suppress the Sendero Luminoso, or Shining Path, rebels led to human-rights violations called "disappearances," people who were taken from their homes or jobs and never seen again.

Peru, whose well-being is vital to the health of the western hemisphere, faces an urgent need to improve its economy, raise the level of education, control the drug trade, and resolve ancient cultural grievances. As it struggles toward these goals, the spectacular ruins of a vast empire—Machu Picchu in particular—attract tens of thousands of visitors yearly. In addition to the viewing of such splendid physical sites, visitors can go back in time by sampling soups made of chuño (dried potato), flavored with the meat of a cui (guinea pig), washed down with chicha (corn beer)—foods of the ancient Inca that still are enjoyed in the highlands.

Importance of the Andean Rain Forest

Loss of rain forests around the world contribute to global warming, a threat to all humankind. Even so, rain forests in Peru's eastern cordillera are harvested for lumber or to clear land for agriculture. The result is severe soil erosion as well as loss of the forest with its diversity of plant and animal life.

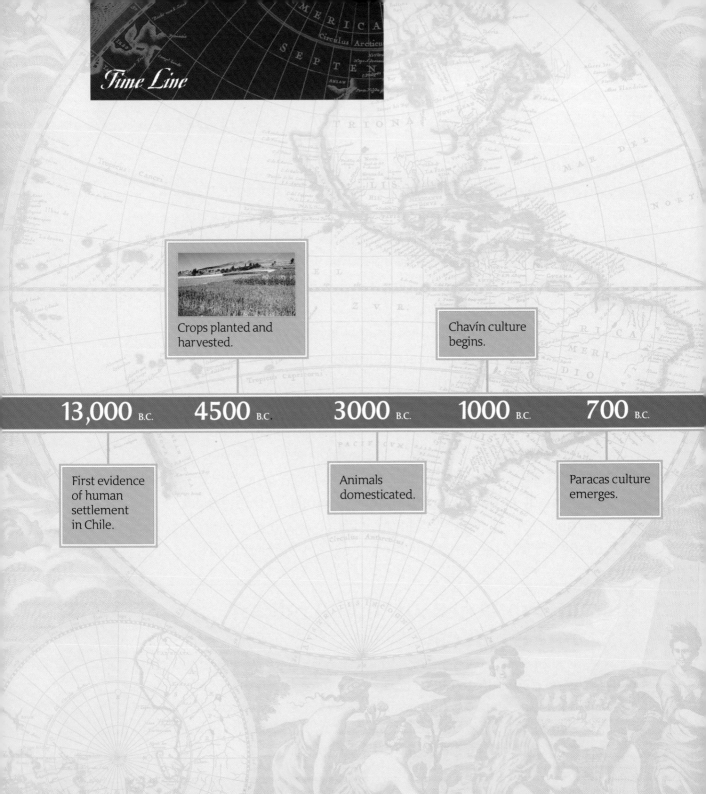

Crops planted and harvested.

Chavín culture begins.

| 13,000 B.C. | 4500 B.C. | 3000 B.C. | 1000 B.C. | 700 B.C. |

First evidence of human settlement in Chile.

Animals domesticated.

Paracas culture emerges.

Nazca, Moche,
Tiahuanaca,
Huari, and
Chimu
cultures arise.

Under Manco Capac,
Inca begin to subdue
neighbors.

Huayna Capac,
eleventh
emperor, takes
the throne.

A.D. 100–900   A.D. **1150–1250**   A.D. **1300**   A.D. **1438**   A.D. **1493**

Inca tribe
settles near
Cuzco.

Pachacuti,
ninth Sapa
Inca, expands
empire.

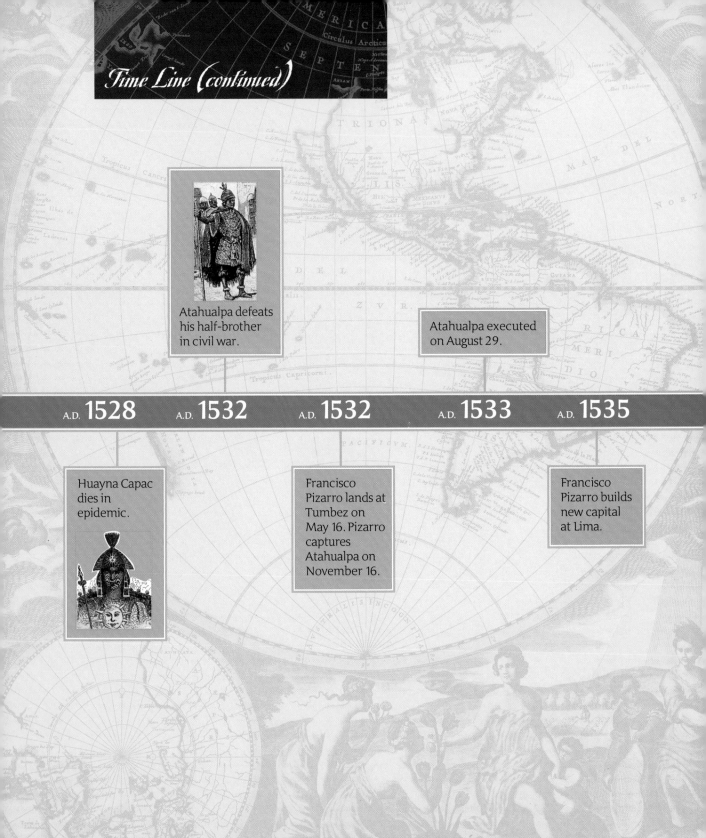

Atahualpa defeats his half-brother in civil war.

Atahualpa executed on August 29.

A.D. **1528**   A.D. **1532**   A.D. **1532**   A.D. **1533**   A.D. **1535**

Huayna Capac dies in epidemic.

Francisco Pizarro lands at Tumbez on May 16. Pizarro captures Atahualpa on November 16.

Francisco Pizarro builds new capital at Lima.

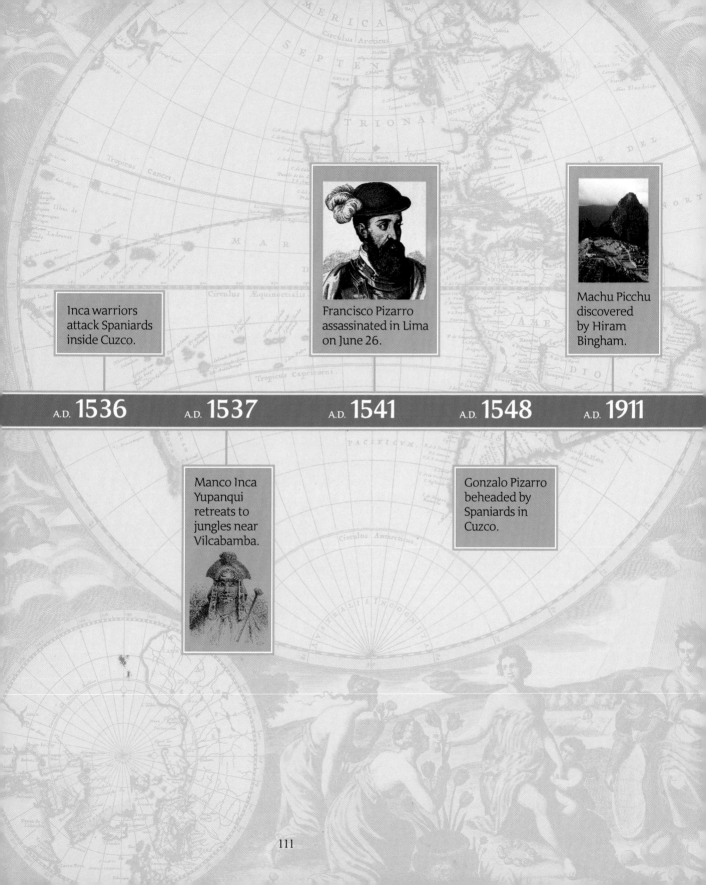

Inca warriors attack Spaniards inside Cuzco.

Francisco Pizarro assassinated in Lima on June 26.

Machu Picchu discovered by Hiram Bingham.

A.D. **1536**   A.D. **1537**   A.D. **1541**   A.D. **1548**   A.D. **1911**

Manco Inca Yupanqui retreats to jungles near Vilcabamba.

Gonzalo Pizarro beheaded by Spaniards in Cuzco.

Atahualpa

1500?–1533

Atahualpa, the eleventh Inca emperor, was not the legitimate heir to the throne. He seized power from his half-brother, Huascar, in "The War of Two Brothers" that ended in 1532. His reign was brief. He was executed by Francisco Pizarro in 1533.

Garcilaso de la Vega

1539–1616

Garcilaso de la Vega's mother was the granddaughter of the tenth Inca emperor. His father was the Spanish governor of Cuzco. He wrote *Royal Commentaries of the Incas*, a memoir of his childhood. It was published in Portugal in 1609.

Huaman Poma de Ayala

c. 1535–1620?

Huaman Poma de Ayala, of Inca descent, adopted the surname of a Spanish army captain. He wrote *The First New Chronicle of Good Government*. It is best known for Ayala's black-and-white drawings depicting daily life among the Inca.

Huascar

1499?–1532

Huascar was the first-born son of Huayna Capac, the eleventh emperor. He was the legitimate heir to the Inca throne. After his father died, his half-brother Atahualpa went to war against him. Atahualpa was victorious and executed Huascar in 1532.

Huayna Capac

Ruled 1493–1528

Huayna Capac, the eleventh Inca emperor, ruled wisely for thirty-four years. At his death, he left the northern province of Quito to his younger son, Atahualpa. His older son Huascar inherited the throne in Cuzco. Rivalry caused the half-brothers to pit themselves against each other.

Manco Inca Yupanqui

Died 1545

Manco Inca Yupanqui was named in honor of the "first Inca" of ancient myth. He became a "puppet emperor" in 1533. After the Spaniards murdered his sister-wife, Manco Inca swore revenge. He besieged the Spaniards in Cuzco for one year. Later he was hunted down and killed at Vilcabamba in the northern part of the empire.

Pachacuti

Ruled 1438–1471

Pachacuti, the ninth Inca emperor, was so powerful that he was called "Earthshaker." He brought many new provinces under Inca rule. He ordered the construction of a stone fortress on a hilltop called Sacsahuamán ("Speckled Hawk") overlooking Cuzco. The project took thirty years to complete and required twenty thousand workers.

Quizquiz

Died 1534

Quizquiz, Atahualpa's best general, escaped the Spanish massacre at Cajamarca in 1532. He fled north to Quito, where he commanded ten thousand Inca warriors. In 1534, after a long battle against the Spaniards, he refused to surrender. His own men, exhausted and hungry, killed him themselves.

Topa Inca Yupanqui

Ruled 1471–1493

Topa Inca Yupanqui, the tenth Inca emperor, was the son of the great Pachacuti. He continued his father's program of subduing every major province in the Andes. The result was the largest empire in the New World. His grandsons—Atahualpa and Huascar—weakened the kingdom by waging war against each other.

Tupac Amaru

Died 1572

Tupac Amaru was one of Manco Inca's three sons. He became the last Inca emperor after his father's death at the the hands of the Spaniards in Vilcabamba. Like his father, he was hunted down and executed.

Tupac Hualpa

Died 1533

Tupac Hualpa was the Spaniards' first choice to be a "puppet emperor" after the conquest. They believed he'd be easy to control. Tupac Hualpa's reign lasted only two months. He was poisoned, reportedly by Inca nobles who remained loyal to Huascar.

Viracocha Inca

Ruled until 1438

Viracocha Inca was the eighth emperor, named in honor of the creator-god, Viracocha. He was a shrewd military leader, adding 150,000 square miles (388,498 sq. km) of territory to the empire.

acllacuna girl picked to live at the House of Chosen Women

acsu wild potato

alcaide mayor

altiplano treeless, grass-covered plain in Andes Mountains

amautas wise men, teachers

apo high government official

aucu warrior

ayllu clan, or kinship unit

Biru river in Colombia, called "Peru" by Spaniards

bola weapon made of three stones tied to llama tendons

capac-nan royal road

chacra field

charqui dried meat

chasquis messengers who ran in relays

chicha corn beer used in Inca celebrations

citua ceremony to rid the empire of disease

collahuaya healer, medicine man

cordillera twin mountain ranges of the Andes

coya emperor's official wife; also his sister

cui a small rodent, also known as a guinea pig

curaca governor; chief of an ethnic group

encomienda land grants given to Spanish settlers in Peru

guano bird droppings; fertilizer

guarachicuy boy's coming-of-age ceremony

hampi-camayoc healer who kept herbs and potions

huaccha concha illegitimate offspring of royalty

huanacauri rainbow

Inca "lord," "only lord," or "unique lord"

Inti the sun

Intip Churín Children of the Sun

intip llocsina "place where the sun springs up"

llamactu Inca government official

lampa small hoe used to plant crops

llanco red clay

llauto headband worn by Inca men

locro potato stew flavored with chili peppers

mamacona older women in House of Chosen Women

matec-llu plant used to treat snow blindness

mestizo person of mixed race

mit'a tax paid by performing labor

mitamaes "people from elsewhere"

molle pepper tree

naupa pacha "in ancient times"

pahuac oncoy epidemic

panaca kinship group of royalty

papa Spanish name for potato

piedras cansadas "weary stones"

Quechua language spoken by the Inca

quechua planting zone between 5,000 feet and 10,000 feet

quicuchicuy girl's coming-of-age ceremony

quina tree whose bark produces quinine

quinoa grain similar to barley

quipu device made of knotted strings, used for counting

quirau baby's cradle

quollas storehouses

rutuchicoy child's hair-cutting ceremony

sayri tobacco, called "holy weed" by Spaniards

suncasapa bearded men

surumpi snow blindness

taclla wooden foot plow

tambos rest stops along highland roads

taqui feast to commemorate the dead

totora coarse, tough reed used to make fishing boats

verruca viral disease of the highlands

wawa baby

Yachahuasi House of Learning, a type of university

yanca ayllu commoners, of common blood

yunga planting zone below 5,000 feet

Books

Chrisp, Peter. *The Incas*. New York: Thomsen Learning, 1994.

de Angelis, Gina. *Francisco Pizarro and the Conquest of the Inca*. Philadelphia: Chelsea House Publishers, 2001.

Drew, David. *Inca Life*. Hauppauge, NY: Barron's Educational Series, Inc., 2000.

Lourie, Peter. *Lost Treasure of the Inca*. Boyds Mills Press, 1999.

Lyle, Garry. *Peru*. Philadelphia: Chelsea House Publishers, 1998.

Macdonald, Fiona. *Inca Town*. Danbury, CT: Franklin Watts, 1999.

Mann, Elizabeth. *Machu Picchu*. New York: Mikaya Press, 2000.

Martell, Hazel Mary. *Civilizations of Peru Before 1535*. Austin, TX: Raintree Steck-Vaughn, 1999.

Nishi, Dennis. *The Inca Empire*. San Diego, CA: Lucent Books, 2000.

Steele, Philip. *Step Into the Inca World*. New York: Lorenz Books, 2000.

Wood, Tim. *The Incas*. New York: Viking, 1996.

Videos

The Incas. PBS Home Video, 1980.

Inca Mummies: Secrets of a Lost World. National Geographic Television, 2002.

Mysteries of Peru: Enigma of the Ruins. Atlas Video Inc., Bethesda, MD, 1993.

Organizations and Online Sites

American Museum of Natural History
Central Park West at 79th Street
New York, NY 10024-5192
http://www.amnh.org

The museum's permanent collection includes art, traditions, architecture of the Inca.

Inca Mummies
http://nationalgeographic/inca

Learn more about the burial practices of the Inca and the process of mummification.

National History Museum of Los Angeles
900 Exposition Boulevard
Los Angeles, CA 90007
http://www.nhm.org/

The museum's Web site offers information and images of its ancient Latin America collection.

Polk Museum of Art
800 East Palmetto Street
Lakeland, Florida 33801-5529
http://www.polkmuseumofart.org

The museum has a collection of pre-Columbian art, including Inca artifacts.

About the Author

Patricia Calvert is an award-winning author of children's nonfiction and fiction. She grew up in Montana, whose mountains are as beautiful in their way as the Andes Mountains of the Inca Empire. She lived in the woods near Big Timber Creek, climbed the mountains that surrounded her house, had a horse, a dog, several cats—even a brother. When she was ten years old, Patricia decided she'd like to be a writer someday. When she was older, she became interested in history, too. History is a special kind of story. It informs us about the world's past and its many people. To learn more about long ago times, Patricia traveled to ancient sites in England, Scotland, Ireland, Greece, Italy, and Mexico. On her next trip she plans to hike the *capac-nam*, the royal road of the ancient Inca.